Women's Legal Struggles After Violence

Jackson De Neeve

Table of Contents

Abstract

Women who have been the victim of violence have always been at a disadvantage under the laws in the United States because these laws stem from a patriarchal, sexist, heteronormative, and racist ideology under which this country was founded. Self- defense laws have shown to be no different and serve as a constraint to women who attempt to protect themselves at the hands of an abuser. This dissertation focuses on women who have been the victim of violence at the hands of an abuser to show that the law is not doing an adequate job of protecting them. It accomplishes this in many ways. First, this Dissertation explores the existing literature to show that the inadequate justice women receive after being the victim of violence is not a new problem and it is, in fact, very well established. Second, a legal analysis is done to show that laws that protect men who defend themselves and those that protect women are not only separate, they are not equal and women are at an extreme disadvantage. Third, a case analysis is done to highlight Black women specifically and show that our system of justice uses many different tools to ensure these women do not receive justice, thereby creating an impossible system to overcome. Finally, interviews were conducted with key actors in the criminal justice system to highlight the ultimate finding that none of these processes work in a vacuum and without major change at every level of justice, these women will continue to be re-victimized by a system that should be working to protect them.

Introduction

The lack of protection for women who have been victims of violence is not a new phenomenon in the United States, especially as it relates to women who have been abused at the hands of an intimate partner. In fact, marital rape in the United States was not even a crime until the 1970s (Bergen & Barnhill 2006). Due to this lack of protection, women are reluctant to tell their stories for fear that they will not be believed and, even worse, will have no recourse.

Understanding the physical, mental, and emotional trauma caused by abuse at the hands of an intimate partner is extremely important for recognizing the legal, moral, and ethical implications caused by the law's failure to protect women. Although there seems to be a lot of research that has been conducted surrounding victims of violence, the work is still not done. Our society must continue to work towards fair and just resolutions for these women. Women must have recourse in the criminal justice arena and be provided with mental and physical health resources. These proposed recourses must support victims while they are coping with experiencing these traumatic events. Therefore, we must develop solutions that value women, their bodies, and their sexuality, in addition to removing the negative stigmas that plague them in all these respects. This includes an examination and restructuring of our laws.

Americans, in general, believe that the victim of a crime should have a right to defend themselves from unwarranted intrusions on their person or property (Fox 2013). Self-defense is a commonly known legal concept applied in many cases, even before its formal codification through statute. Since 2005, however, we have seen self-defense statutes expanded in many ways, but most of these ways do nothing to protect women adequately.

Over the last 20 years, the laws protecting individuals who choose to defend themselves against an attack have become increasingly broad. This means the law is expanding to protect more individuals after they use force against another person. Often these individuals are not in danger, but they perceive a threat or claim that they perceive a threat. They are still protected. There is currently much debate over whether these laws are fair or give individuals a right to murder and still be covered under the law (McClellan, C. & Tekin, E. 2017). Most of the situations we have seen thus far involve males who do not know each other, which explains why they can perceive danger and be justified. (McClellan, C. & Tekin, E. 2017)

But what do we do in situations involving two individuals that are not strangers but are also, in fact, lovers? What if that "love" was not love at all, only had a physical manifestation, and was based on coercion? Our laws do little to protect women in situations of these types of abuse. This is an institutional problem. Research has shown that the ways women react to abuse are different in many ways from the traditional legal articulations of justified self-defense (Walklate, S., Fitz-Gibbon, K., & McCulloch, J. 2018).

This dissertation explores the ways our self-defense laws have evolved concurrently while we are learning more about the responses of women who have been victims of violence. Are we doing enough to protect them? If not, what could we do better? How are our self-defense laws evolving? Do women have the same access to self-defense laws as men? How can our statutes be tailored to ensure these women have better protection from domestic violence?

Definitions

For this dissertation's purposes, the arguments presented will focus on all types of physical violence, including sexual, intimate partner, and domestic violence. Sexual violence involves any act of unwanted sexual activity, but usually consists of sexually motivated violence. Domestic violence describes violence enacted by one or more family members against another (Johnson 2011). It can involve physical and sexual violence, but also non-physical acts such as manipulation and economic or emotional abuse and is usually what we think of when we see women seeking help from a partner (Johnson 2011).

Intimate Partner Violence (IPV) encompasses many types of violence between couples. While domestic violence is one type of IPV, most instances of IPV are usually caused by a specific situation or event (Johnson 2011). In other words, sexual violence is one form of domestic violence, and domestic violence is one form of IPV; however, IPV includes more types of violence than just domestic violence and can happen based on one situation, one time (Johnson 2011). It is also important to note that IPV does not include violence done in self-defense as protection. The term for that is defensive violence and this dissertation advocates that women should be allowed to use defensive violence when appropriate, and the law should do more to protect them in these situations.

The research will include scenarios in which women have previously been the victim of physical violence and are now faced with a threat of violence, because, as I demonstrate, many women may not immediately respond to violence and may only turn to self-defense after years of abuse or in the direst circumstances[1]. This includes, in some instances, statutory rape.

Also, for this dissertation, the arguments presented will focus on relationships between women and men. This is because there are not very many cases of same-sex couples in this situation. Therefore, current data surrounding same-sex couples in the criminal justice system is much more limited. This could be, in part, because same-sex couples report instances of violence less (Gerstenberger, C., Stansfield, R. & Williams, K.R. 2019; Alexander, C.J. 2002). Additionally, in the interviews conducted, the practitioners had limited to no experience in dealing with same-sex couples. This supports the argument that will be presented later in this dissertation that the laws are based on white, heteronormative principles of relationships, and same-sex relationships give additional variables that are outside of the scope of the capacity of the criminal justice system. Future research should include studies on this issue.

Additionally, this dissertation will focus on individuals who know each other or have encountered each other on more than one occasion. Although I will present cases involving strangers who met each other one time, those cases are older and are used to contrast present law from the law of that time. I submit that the current law does more to protect women in situations with strangers because the courts recognize the danger as "imminent." Whereas the law provides some protection for women in such situations, this dissertation particularly argues for legal solutions that address cases in which the violent encounter is not presently happening, even if one of the parties simply leaves to get a weapon and immediately returns.

Finally, it is essential to remember that there are at least two sides to each of these stories, and part of the problem is that women are not believed. After a careful reading of the cases, court opinions, the law, and the historical legacy of institutional misogyny, I have taken the ethical position to believe that women are telling the truth, something that is rarely done in the court system. Further, I use the words "victim" and "defendant" interchangeably for many of these women, and it is essential to remember that in many of these cases, both are correct since the victim of violence later becomes the defendant in court.

Theoretical Framework

Throughout this research, I will be using multiple theoretical frameworks to examine the literature. The theoretical frameworks were chosen based on the commonly used frameworks in the literature that is cited below. The dominant theoretical framework that will be used throughout this research is the feminist perspective. Through this perspective, the goal is to illuminate and eliminate the factors that lead to inequality, oppression, and injustice. Doing this then promotes the pursuit of equality and justice. The goal of this research is to illustrate the traumatic experiences of women after they experience violence, which fits squarely within the feminist framework. More specifically, this research will use critical race and critical feminist theory to reexamine the literature related to the topic and identify gaps within the processes as well as within the literature. I will look at gender violence in addition to being critical of the legal system and its operations.

The other framework I will use throughout this research is the interpretivist framework. The interpretivist framework accepts that "we live in a world of potentially multiple, intersubjective social realities in which the researcher (as well as the researched) is also an interpreter of events that transpire and sometimes an actor in them..." (Swartz & Yanow 2013, pp. 41). This research will focus on the experiences of different people within the system, their trauma after the violence, and how that trauma develops. To do this, we must interpret many thoughts, opinions, and perceptions. However, it is within these interpretations that we find the answers to our research questions. Most research involving women who have been the victim of violence that has been done already looks through an interpretivist lens, so this research falls squarely in line with the already existing research.

Argument

As stated earlier, research suggests women who are the victim of violence are either not heard or not believed, a phenomenon that has been referred to as "the credibility discount" (Tuerkheimer, D. 2017, pp. 3). The reasons for this unfortunate fact come from various places, including the misconception that women falsely report abuse and sexual violence, the stigma placed on women for the abuse that happens to them (Epstein, D. & Goodman, L. A. 2018), and patriarchal, heteronormative ideas of men dominating women's bodies. This is important to note because Florida's most recent self-defense law has become commonly referred to as "Stand Your Ground" (SYG) and relies entirely on the credibility of witnesses in most instances.

Florida's SYG law is codified in the Florida Statutes, specifically Section 776. Although there are a few variations in that statute, the overarching principle is that a person is justified in defending themself "to the extent that the person reasonably believes that such conduct is necessary to defend himself or herself or another" (Fla. Stat. 776.012(1)). This law applies a "reasonableness" standard when determining whether the use of deadly force is justified. That means that the trier of fact, either the judge or the jury (depending on the stage of the proceedings), must determine whether the defendant acted in a way that was justified given the situation.

By making this law based on a "reasonableness" standard, victims are required to prove they were in fear, in addition to proving that they were actual victims of sexual, physical, or other violence. That is a burden that many victims will have no proof of other than their own words, and even if they could prove it through words alone, the burden is so high that many victims will not want to go through the stress because the weight of proving their credibility introduces additional trauma (Freedman, A.E. 2002). Considering all these situations, how much are we really protecting these women?

One problem with this law, when it applies to victims of violence, is the word "imminent." According to Merriam-Webster's dictionary, the term "imminent" means "ready to take place: happening soon." What we see many times with victims of sexual violence is that their response to the violence is not imminent, at least not in the ways the courts define this law, though, for the women who endure chronic abuse, the violence may always be imminent. Oftentimes women cannot defeat their attacker in a direct confrontation, and other times, when women decide to retaliate, it is because they are responding to a consistent stimulus with an onset of post-traumatic stress disorder, and they just "snap" (Crisafi 2016).

In either of those scenarios, the threat of violence is not imminent according to the courts (*Gaffney v. State*, 742 So. 2d 358, 360 (Fla. Dist. Ct. App. 1999); *State v. Woodson*, 349 So. 3d 510 (Fla. Dist. Ct. App. 2022). However, it is essential to mention that "imminent" is not actually defined by the Legislature in Fla. Stat. Chapter 776, nor in the definitions. It is also not described by the Supreme Court of Florida in the standard jury instructions. Therefore, the courts have used their own definitions that they arrived at based on the dictionary. Most recently, the Fifth District quoted Miriam Webster by saying that an imminent act is one that is "ready to take place: happening soon." *(State v. Woodson 2022; Miriam-Webster 2022).* "Soon" could have been interpreted by the courts to mean that the action was happening in a few days, weeks, months, or years, thereby providing protection to these women. However, thus far, we have not seen this happening, and, as this dissertation will illustrate, in most instances, juries do not interpret it that way either. Because the law is ambiguous and leaves this word up for interpretation, women are left unprotected from the patriarchal stereotypes based on a lack of affording credibility to women that still exists in society today. If the legislature or courts chose to define imminence in a way that accounts for these types of situations, more women could be protected under the law.

For these reasons, what we will see is that many women may find themselves in situations where they must defend themselves from their attacker, and when they finally decide to stand up for themselves, they must protect themselves from the legal system as well. This result is not fair, nor is it just. Therefore, our criminal justice system must reconsider the way it handles situations such as these.

Further, this dissertation will illustrate that even changes in the law will not fix this issue because the law is social and political (West 1995; Ladson-Billings, G. 2021). There is no equality under the law, only the administration of the law (Sekhon, N. 2019). Hence, changing one fact, for example, the defendant being white versus black or male versus female—can create disparate outcomes, even when the law seems entirely neutral on its face. Therefore, until our system of justice undergoes a meaningful change, it can never evolve.

Significance of Study

This study contributes to our understanding of the vulnerability of women to violence, both prior to and during their engagement with the criminal legal system. It does this in several ways. First, and possibly most important, there has been little research done related to SYG laws and how they specifically apply to women who have been victims of violence. By addressing this gap, we will be able to see the actual effects of this failure to provide legal recourse out of abusive relationships for women and whether the laws have an unequal impact on women who have been victims of violence.

Second, this study takes an interdisciplinary approach and looks at these cases from multiple perspectives. It combines public policy with gender (and possibly race) studies, legal studies, and criminology. An interdisciplinary approach is necessary because the issues presented in this dissertation do not fit squarely in any one discipline and require a concerted effort to encompass the sources of conflict given and propose a solution.

Third, and most generally, this study contributes to the literature related to women who have been victims of violence to illuminate their vulnerability because of the law. In doing this, we can hopefully identify barriers that contribute to the inadequate justice these women are receiving in the legal system. By identifying such obstacles, we can develop more critical, and even impactful, ways to provide women with additional avenues for redress and protection.

Organization of Dissertation

This dissertation consists of four substantive chapters followed by conclusions. Chapter One will discuss existing literature related to Battered Woman Syndrome (BWS), Intimate Partner Violence (IPV), and SYG laws to provide the current understanding as it relates to women who have been victims of violence and self-defense laws. Chapter Two will review the history of SYG laws in Florida, starting with the Castle Doctrine and moving through BWS and SYG laws to illustrate that the BWS and SYG laws have evolved to create separate discourses for men and women based on the same type of crime. Chapter Three will take a closer look at Black women throughout the history United States who have been the victim of physical violence and the ways that they have been treated by the criminal justice system to illustrate that these laws disadvantages women, but Black women through many different arbitrary avenues of justice administration. Further, in many instances, these women face additional challenges because they are both Black and women. Therefore, the chapter will take an intersectional approach to understand the ways these women have not only been silenced but erased.

In Chapter Four, I present and analyze interviews with prosecutors, defense attorneys, victim advocates, judges, a professor, and legislative advocates to try to understand better the many barriers at multiple levels that women face as defendants in self-defense cases. In concert with my initial presentation of the legislative theory and history surrounding self-defense laws, my discussion of BWS as an inadequate defense device, my analyses of specific cases of self-defense in nineteenth and twentieth-century U.S. case law, and my attention to the vulnerabilities against Back women, these interviews provide three main takeaways. First, the bias against all women and especially against Black women, will not be remedied under the existing system. Second, changing the law may have some effect, but existing cases demonstrate that arbitrariness and bias are still embedded in the system. Third, because the law does not administer itself, actors, including justices, attorneys, and juries, are forced to operate in a system embedded with institutional racism and sexism against women, even when individual actors educate themselves.

This dissertation will show that women, especially Black women, are disadvantaged under our current laws related to self-defense. It seems like the rights of White men continue to expand under SYG laws, and the rights of women are continuously being limited by a lack of understanding and trust of victims. This fact becomes even more detrimental when the intersection of Black and women are combined. Although the problem has been identified repeatedly, without significant systematic change, women who have been the victims of violence will continue to be abused, silenced, and erased by our system of justice.

Chapter One: Literature Review

This dissertation addresses Florida's current self-defense laws and how they do not protect women who have been victims of physical violence. To fully understand these laws and the gaps that exist within, we must first examine the relevant literature on the topics of IPV, BWS, and SYG laws, in addition to all pertinent literature related to how the three areas overlap to determine what existing scholarship says about women who have been victims of physical violence and their interactions with the criminal justice system.

Before SYG laws, many states had laws that afforded limited protection to women. First, through the Castle Doctrine. Then, as women began gaining rights through the women's rights movement, Lenore Walker, a psychologist, produced the term "Battered Woman Syndrome" to describe the psychological effects abuse had on women. (Walker 1979). BWS is a psychological condition with effects like post-traumatic-stress disorder that occurs as a response from women who have been the victim of repeated violence, usually physical, in an intimate relationship (Rivers-Schutte 2013). Even before this term was established, cases involving women who had been the victim of violence were referred to as this condition, though it was not explicitly called "Battered Woman Syndrome" (Rivers-Schutte 2013; Schneider E.M. 1986). For example, one of the first successful assertions of a legal defense based on a woman suffering at the hands of domestic abuse in the twentieth-century U.S. involved Francine Hughes. The incident occurred on March 29, 1977, and involved a woman who had been battered for 13 years at the hands of her husband and then decided to set his bed on fire while he was sleeping after enduring his abuse for the last time (Musselman, M. & Sorrentino, R. 2019; Grimes 2017). Instead of using the BWS defense, she pled temporary insanity and was found not guilty by a jury (Musselman, M. & Sorrentino, R. 2019; Grimes 2017).

Since the implementation of BWS as a defense, advocates for the inclusion of violence against men have brought attention to the fact that the term "domestic violence" is not inclusive. To ensure the inclusion of both men and women and to also include those who have been the victim of abuse that may not have been physical, the term "Intimate Partner Violence" has been developed and is technically more accurate (although for purposes of this dissertation, the group we are discussing includes only women). The CDC (Centers for Disease Control) defines IPV as "physical violence, sexual violence, stalking, or psychological harm by a current or former partner or spouse. This type of violence can occur among heterosexual or same-sex couples and does not require sexual intimacy" (Centers for Disease Control, 2021). In short, BWS occurs when women who have repeatedly been victims of IPV.

Defenses provided to women who have been victims of IPV have not been perfect. Still, they acknowledge the violence between partners in relationships and offer a potential remedy to give justice to the real victims in these situations. However, in Florida in 2005, the laws that provide protection specifically for individuals in relationships were primarily subsumed by a more general law known as SYG. Florida became the first State to adopt a law that expressly stated that individuals in fear of imminent "great bodily harm or death" have no duty to retreat and therefore have the right to "stand their ground." Since SYG laws are so general, the objective is to provide legal protection in self-defense scenarios to potential victims of the crime and the need to defend themselves. In sum, women who are the victim of IPV can then experience BWS, which may cause them to use violence against their abusive partners. In Florida, if charges are filed against them related to the offense, they use a BWS defense to support the "reasonableness requirement" under the SYG law.

Overview of Violence Against Women (General)

The point of this dissertation is to explore laws relating to victims of physical violence, whether the defense they use in court is BWS or SYG, or whether the type of violence is referred to as domestic violence or IPV. Before discussing specific defenses and legal terms, it is essential to start with the basics. This first section explores existing literature surrounding women who have been victims of violence. Before we can understand whether the existing laws do enough to protect these women, we need to have a broader idea of who these women are; and although they are in no way a homogeneous group, learning about the specific qualities and trauma that they experience will help to lay the groundwork for understanding the legal processes that relate to them.

Violence Against Women (VAW) is defined by the United Nations as "any act of gender-based violence that results in, or is likely to result in, physical, sexual or psychological harm or suffering to women, including threats of such acts, coercion or arbitrary deprivation of liberty, whether occurring in public or in private life." (U.N. General Assembly 1993; Dillon, G., Hussain, R., Loxton, D., & Rahman, S. 2013). Physical violence consists of aggressive actions, including pushing, hitting, biting, punching, slapping, kicking, beating, and other things that cause injury or death to someone (Ellsberg, M. et al. 1999; Krantz, G., & Garcia-Moreno, C. 2005). "Sexual assault" is a term that refers to the use of "force, coercion, or an imbalance of power to make a person engage in sexual activity without their consent" (Planned Parenthood, 2023). "Rape" includes vaginal, anal, or oral penetration or attempted penetration by the offender using coercion or force. (Sinozich, S. & Langton, L. 2014). The CDC is much more inclusive in its definition and uses the term "sexual violence" instead of "sexual assault." "Sexual violence" includes:

[C]ompleted or attempted penetration of the genital opening or anus by the penis, a hand, a finger, or any other object, or penetration of the mouth by the penis or other object. Sexual violence also includes non-penetrative abusive sexual contact (e.g., intentional touching of the groin), as well as non-contact sexual abuse (e.g., voyeurism, exposure to pornography) (Basile & Saltzman 2002).

Also, according to the CDC, "[S]exual violence occurs when the victim does not consent to the sexual activity, or when the victim is unable to consent (e.g., due to age, illness) or refuse (e.g., due to physical violence or threats)" (Basile & Saltzman 2002).

This is not all-inclusive of all types of VAW. Of all the forms of VAW, psychological abuse is the most difficult to define validly and reliably (Follingstad 2007; Jordan, Campbell, and Follingstad 2010). Although recently, more researchers have discovered new scales to increase the scientific validity of these findings (Ureña, J et al. 2015). Stalking is also considered a form of VAW (Jordan, Campbell, and Follingstad, 2010). However, in either of those two scenarios, an individual would not be justified in using physical violence in self-defense under existing laws. Therefore, we will focus on the scenarios which COULD (in theory) allow someone to use justifiable force, which, for the purposes of this dissertation, will be physical and sexual VAW.

The History of VAW

Before the Civil war, Americans defined manhood primarily as the man's ability to maintain control over his family (Ross 2015). This is not surprising since Western culture typically categorized women's bodies as property belonging to men (Weitz & Weitz 2016; Ross 2015). Further, in some ancient cultures, there was no regard given to women or their bodies, who were not even seen as persons (Weitz & Weitz 2016). The women belonged to their fathers before marriage and then to their husbands. The fact that (White) men had the right to control their "property," including their wives, with almost no oversight from the government created a culture in which men could do whatever they wanted with their wives without having to fear being punished by the law (Ross 2015). This status was based on the belief that women's bodies were different from men and these differences caused women's bodies to be both defective and, in many ways, dangerous; therefore, needing to be controlled by men (Weitz & Weitz 2016). Further,

Biblical interpretations led society to believe that it was a divine right for men to rule over women (Jones 2008; Wood, H. J. 2019).

But by the antebellum era, advocates were bringing more attention to violence between intimate partners, and after the Civil War, the country started to worry more about violence between them. During the time of change in the 1870s and 1880s, the new attack on IPV gave black and white women the same legal and social protections. However, the violence still had to be extreme in public and the result of intoxication before legal action would be taken. Private instances of violence still were not subject to discipline. (Baggett 2017; Siegel 1995)

Nevertheless, at the turn of the twentieth century, any progress toward reform in IPV had regressed. There was a significant push toward the family structure. IPV took a back seat to family preservation because of race-dominated issues in the South. Biologists cautioned against the expanding rights of women, stating that as a result, the family and the entire country will suffer. The establishment of family courts, which would determine the effects of cases of IPV, was lobbied for by social workers. The overarching principles promoted the family at all costs and preserved traditional ideas of what it meant to be a woman, thereby effectively decriminalizing abuse. Even in the early 1900s, wife beating was recommended as "proper discipline" (Waugh 1913, *cited by* Baggett 2017). (Baggett 2017)

This view prevailed until the women's rights movement, and even then, change was slow and happened over a long time. For example, the legal recourse for most women suffering from abuse would have been a divorce, and although it was not the case in most states, women in South Carolina could not get divorced until the 1940s, and women in New York were only allowed to be divorced in cases of adultery until the late 1960s (Ross 2015). In 1971, the Supreme Court of the United States, in *Reed v. Reed*, 404 U.S. 71 (1971), held that differential treatment based on sex was illegal (Weitz, R. & Weitz, R 2016). However, even after this time, women were fighting an uphill battle. It was not until 1984 that any court convicted a man for raping a woman to whom he was still legally married and living in the same house (Weitz, R. & Weitz, R 2016). In reviewing this history, it becomes clear that not much has changed for women in the last 50 years because of the pre-existing barriers to equality that were set in place at the inception of western society. However, this mistreatment of women has significant implications. (Weitz, R. & Weitz, R 2016)

Effects of VAW

Some studies that have explored the physical health effects of VAW show that these effects can constitute significant health issues for these victims (e.g., Coker et al. 2000; García-Moreno, C. et al. 2013). Domestic violence has been linked to depression and anxiety disorders (Knight, L., & Hester, M. 2016; Fisher, B. & Regan, S. 2006). Additionally, many studies have linked domestic violence to an increased likelihood of experiencing post-traumatic stress disorder (O'Campo, P. et al. 2006; Trevillion et al. 2012; Dillon et al. 2013; Chmielowska, M. & Fuhr, D.C. 2017; Chandan et al. 2020). In addition to PTSD (Post Traumatic Stress Disorder), anxiety, and depression, IPV has also been linked to drug and alcohol abuse, suicidality, self-harm, and suicidal thoughts and feelings (Koss et al. 2003; Romito et al. 2005; World Health Organization 2013; Jonas et al. 2014; Moulding et al. 2021). There is also a significant connection between IPV and psychosis and eating disorders (Jonas et al. 2014).

Several other studies show that certain aspects of a victimization event are linked to the severity of the psychological effects that follow. For example, PTSD effects are more likely (and worse) when there is a threat to life, an injury, a lot of force used, and incredibly invasive acts (Housecamp, B.M. & Foy, D.W. 1991; Pill, N., Day, A., & Mildred, H. 2017). Further, the frequency, severity, duration, and recentness of interpersonal victimization have been linked to higher levels of psychological distress, such as PTSD, anxiety, depression, and other symptoms (Housecamp, B.M. & Foy, D.W. 1991; Goodman, L. A., Dutton, M. A., & Harris, M. 1997; Pill, N., Day, A., & Mildred, H. 2017).

Violence against women is also associated with physical ailments. For example, some studies claim that physical interactions between intimate partners can cause bruising, cuts, fractured bones, contusions, head injuries, and internal wounds (Sutherland, C. A., Bybee, D. I.,

& Sullivan, C. M. 2002; Lutgendorf 2019). Respiratory conditions (Loxton, D. et al. 2006), musculoskeletal conditions (Woods et al. 2008), cardiovascular disorders (Loxton, D. et al. 2006; Nur, N. 2012), diabetes (Nur, N. 2012), breathing difficulties (Loxton 2006), fatigue (Woods et al. 2008), and gastrointestinal symptoms (Drossman 1999) have all been found to be linked to IPV (Dillon, G., Hussain, R., Loxton, D., & Rahman, S. 2013). IPV has also been related to chronic pain, including headaches, insomnia, and pelvic pain (Wuest et al. 2008; Lutgendorf 2019), issues with the immune system (Constantino et al. 2000; Garcia-Linares et al. 2004), and changes in inflammatory responses (Newton et al. 2011). IPV can have adverse effects on reproductive health, including miscarriages, gynecologic diseases, unintended pregnancies, early labor, and delivery (Bramhankar, M., & Reshmi, R. S. 2021). Studies have also found additional physical effects, including difficulty walking, dizziness, memory loss, difficulty with daily activities, and vaginal discharge (Ellsberg M. et al., 2008; Lacey et al., 2013). (Stöckl, H., & Penhale, B. 2015)

IPV

In 1976 the National Organization for Women (NOW) decided to make violence against women a priority. They formed a task force and were able to obtain government funds to conduct research and develop additional protection for women through shelters. As the issue became more pressing, NOW, and other feminist organizations were able to join and improve social services for battered wives and changes in legal status to protect women. This led to the law known as the Violence Against Women Act (VAWA), which passed in 1994 with bipartisan support. (National Organization for Women, 2023).

As stated earlier, IPV, as a term, was established to be inclusive. It usually involves situational violence, but can also include domestic violence, which is based on coercive control (Johnson 2011) This means that IPV encompasses many types of violence, not just physical violence. IPV includes:

Physical violence, such as slapping, hitting, kicking, and beating; sexual violence, including forced sexual intercourse and other forms of sexual coercion; emotional (psychological) abuse, such as insults, belittling, constant humiliation, intimidation (e.g., destroying things), threats of harm, threats to take away children; and controlling behaviors, including isolating a person from family and friends; monitoring their movements; and restricting access to financial resources, employment, education or medical care. (World Health Organization, n.d.).

Since there are many distinct types of IPV, there are various levels of severity. The World Health Organization (WHO) defines IPV as follows: "Level I abuse pushing, shoving, grabbing, throwing objects to intimidation or damage to property, and pets; Level II abuse: kicking, biting, and slapping; and Level III: use of a weapon, choking, or attempt to strangulate" (World Health Organization 2012).

Characteristics of Victims of IPV

Many studies have been done to explore the characteristics that lead to IPV in a variety of scenarios. Before going into detail, here are some of the commonly accepted characteristics victims of IPV may share. A woman's greater likelihood of experiencing violence by her partner(s) has been related to several individual risk variables, and these risk factors have been found to be consistent across a variety of circumstances. These include a low level of education (Kryiacou et al. 2017; Yakubovich et al. 2018), exposure to violence between parents (Bazargan-Hejazi et al. 2014), sexual abuse as children, (WHO/LSHTM 2010), and witnessing other forms of abuse (Krug et al. 2002; World Health Organization, 2012). Other studies have also found depression, high impulsivity, a lack of self-control, and alcohol/drug abuse to be included in these factors (Schafer et al., 2004; Stuart, G.L. & Holtzworth-Munroe, 2005; Bazargan-Hejazi et al. 2014)

There are also many related factors that can be determinative of whether a woman is at risk of VAW. These factors include the woman's financial dependence (Chan, K.L. 2009; Tiwari, A. et al. 2007), although other studies have challenged this conclusion (e.g., Brownridge et al. 2008), unhappiness or fighting in the relationship (WHO/LSHTM 2010), males engaging in polygamous relationships (Abramsky, T. et al. 2011), patriarchal relationships (Taft, C.T. et al. 2009; Walker

1979), and women having a higher level of education than her male partner (Kaukinen, C. 2004; World Health Organization 2012).

Community and societal factors include gender-inequitable social norms (especially those that link notions of manhood to dominance and aggression, poverty (Capaldi 2012; Kryiacou et al. 2017), laws that fail to punish IPV within marriages, laws that do not provide for fundamental rights of women in marriage and divorce, and societal approval of violence coupled with elevated levels of violence within the community (Heise & Garcia 2002).

A commonly debated issue in IPV is whether city type, that is, urban, rural, or suburban, plays a role. Research suggests that although IPV rates are similar across locations, homicides related to IPV and some other limited forms may be higher in rural areas than urban ones, and multiracial women, along with separated/divorced women, may be more at risk in rural areas than urban areas (Edwards 2015). These statistics could be attributed to IPV victims in rural areas having less access to IPV services than those in urban areas (Lanier & Maume, 2009; Edwards 2015) because populations in rural areas tend to prefer less governmental interference in their lives (Websdale, N. & Johnson, B. 1998; Logan et al., 2005a) and because these populations tend to show lower support for victims of IPV (Eastman & Bunch 2007). (Edwards 2015)

Overall, there seems to be a lot of research related to what type of women are or are not victims of IPV. Still, the argument lingers about whether it is helpful to try to characterize victims of IPV at all. While this research may be beneficial in identifying signs of women who may have been the victim, it is not helpful, and in many cases, is damaging if it causes women who do not fit these characteristics to be excluded, or, even worse, to be blamed for a "crime" where, under other circumstances, they would be understood to be acting justifiably.

Explanation of Responses from Victims of Violence

Women have many ways of coping with violence. Some retaliate and use physical force to defend themselves, others do not, and the third group of women combines the two ways. During a single instance of violence, multiple techniques are usually used. However, the strategy taken by most women is resistance, but the process that is most helpful is creating a safety plan. (Anderson, et.al., 2014).

Women's safety strategies in response to IPV can be categorized into six distinct types, including:

1) 1) placating, which consists of strategies meant to change the abuser's behavior without confronting him (e.g., trying not to cry during violence), 2) resistance, which consists of strategies meant to change the abuser's behavior as well as shift the balance of power by challenging his perception of control (e.g., fighting back physically), 3) safety planning, which consists of strategies meant to increase resources and choices for leaving or reducing the risk of future violence (e.g., working out an escape plan), 4) legal, which consists of strategies meant to alter the abuser's behavior by using the legal system (e.g., calling police), 5) formal network, which consists of strategies meant to alter the abuser's behavior or increase resources and choices for leaving through the use of public agencies (non-legal; e.g., staying in a shelter), and 6) informal network, which consists of strategies meant to increase resources and choices for leaving or reducing the risk of future violence (e.g., talking with family) (Parker & Gielen 2014; Goodman et al. 2003).

Other strategies consist of cognitive coping, which involves the victim's internal acceptance (Rizo 2015) and violence (Ditcher et al. 2018). Women use different methods at various times throughout abusive relationships, depending on available resources and where she is in the cycle of abuse (Parker & Gielden 2014; Hayes, B.E. 2013).

There is research to suggest that women may use violence to resist coercion and control (Dutton & Goodman 2005), as a survival or protective strategy (Stuart et al. 2006a), to "assert their dignity" (Larance & Miller 2016), to express rage or frustration (Stuart et al. 2006b; Miller & Meloy 2006; Neal et al. 2015), to exact revenge (Neal et al. 2015), or because of other conflict or communication issues in the relationship (Jewkes 2002) (Ditcher et al. 2018;). Unfortunately, women who use violence are more likely to suffer injuries, endure more abuse, and see the severity of the violence escalate, even though it can be employed as a form of protection and defense (Leonard et al. 2014; Whitaker et al. 2007). However, some women may resort to violence as a form of self-defense because other options, including calling the police or finding shelter, are either unavailable to them or will only make their predicament worse (Kennedy et al., 2012; Richie 2012; Ditcher & Rhodes 2011). Other factors, including a woman's substance abuse, can also make women's use of violence as a coping mechanism worse (Cafferky et al. 2016).

Over time, the duration of an abusive relationship might alter a woman's coping strategies. Research suggests that the longer a woman is in a relationship, the more committed she will be to making it work, especially if the abuse does not emerge until later in the relationship (Rusbult & Martz 1995). Some families suffer from "common couple violence," which is violence that does not happen frequently but does happen occasionally; while other families deal with constant violence, "patriarchal terrorism," which is usually at the hands of the male in the relationship and based on the notion of men having the "right" to control their women (Johnson 1995).

Another factor influencing a woman's selection of coping techniques will be the results she obtained from utilizing that strategy in the past. Women are more likely to reuse resources that are perceived to be helpful and less likely to use resources that they deem to be unhelpful. The helpfulness of the aid is often determined by its perceived credibility and availability. (Fleming & Resick 2016).

The perception of the situation's controllability is another element influencing coping mechanisms. According to research on the use of professional vs. personal resources, women used professional resources when they felt like the violence was out of their control, while women used personal resources when they believed that the cause of the violence was not permanent and could be fixed. (Fleming & Resick 2016)

IPV During the COVID-19 pandemic

A more recent area that is important to mention is IPV during the Covid-19 pandemic. The dynamics of IPV were significantly altered during the pandemic as more couples were required to stay home. IPV incidents increased along with the severity of the injuries, and help-seeking behaviors decreased (Gosangi, B. et al. 2021; Evans, M.L. et al. 2020). This could be due, in part, to stay-at-home orders requiring victims and abusers to spend more time in a home together (Buttell, F., & Ferreira, R. J. 2020; World Health Organization 2020). Further, this time at home meant women could not safely call for help during these incidents (Evans, M.L. et al. 2020). Although, other countries did experience an increase in calls to the domestic violence hotline during the beginning of the pandemic when there was a worldwide shelter-in-place order (Agüero, J. 2021). Other notable stressors included unemployment, usually by men, homeschooling children, and health stressors related to the pandemic (Kaukinen 2020). Research has clearly indicated the negative impact of stay-at-home orders and the dangers it causes for IPV victims. Therefore, future research should focus on how to provide safety planning to victims who are forced to stay at home with their abusers, whether through a stay-at-home order, illness, or unemployment.

Women as Aggressors

Although this dissertation centers around women who have been the victim of IPV, there is a well-established body of literature to support the notion that women can also be aggressors in these incidents (Belanger, C. et al. 2015; Carmo, R. et al. 2011; Caldwell, J.E. et al. 2009). One study even found that men are more often the victims of IPV than women (Hoff, B.H. 2012), even though others suggest that is not true (Carmo, R. et al. 2011; Tarzia, L. et al. 2020). It is also possible that current research methods are rooted in the male-perpetrator female-victim framework, thereby ignoring the possibility of gender symmetry in IPV (Carlyle, K.E. et al. 2014).

However, the methods of violence used by men and women seem to differ. The types of violence employed by individuals also vary. There are studies to support the position that women use more severe physical IPV, the family violence perspective (Melton, H.C. & Sillito, C.L. 2012), and studies that suggest men use more severe IPV, the feminist perspective (Caldwell, J.E. et al. 2012). However, the research can be categorized as inconclusive as there are no consistent findings, and multiple studies have inconsistent results (Hamberger, E. K. & Larsen, S. E. 2015).

This issue tends to be understudied because men do not seek help in situations of IPV as much as women (Tsang, W.W.H. 2015). Men who do seek help have more success through family members, mental health providers, and therapy, while they have the most minor success through domestic violence services (Douglas, E. & Hines, D. 2011). More research is needed to understand the effects of IPV on male victims so that better treatment methods can be obtained (Tarzia, L. et al., 2020).

Another issue that is not well settled relates to the differences between men and women as it relates to IPV. Some research suggests that men and women report using IPV in self-defense equally (Leisring & Grigorian 2016; Harned 2001). Even further, one study suggests that men and women reported committing IPV for the same reasons: difficulties communicating, self-defense, and to express negative emotions (Elmquist et al. 2014; Shorey et al. 2010).

BWS

As noted previously, BWS refers to the psychological repercussions suffered by women who are victims of VAW and, more specifically, IPV. The "tension building" part of BWS consists of the man harassing the woman, convincing her that she is worthless, and making her dependent on him. The second stage is actual physical abuse, which can take several forms. The final phase is referred to as "loving contrition," where the man lavishes the woman with love and devotion and convinces her that the abuse will stop. In some instances, there is no loving contrition, only a phase of no tension. These three phases are repeated until the victim feels unworthy of love and is forced to stay with the abuser. It is a myth that every battered woman experiences all three of these stages, and relationships take many different forms. For example, in the most violent relationships, the last phase may no longer exist. (Walker, L.E. 1979; Walker, L.E. 1984).

Court Processes and Their Effects on Victims

Police involvement is critical to the IPV cycle, particularly in breaking the cycle and protecting the victims (Knudson, J. 2005). Typically, a victim's first interaction with the criminal justice system will be with a responding officer who takes a report (Patterson, D. 2011). A detective is then tasked with investigating the crime and interviewing the victim and suspect (Patterson, D. 2011). Studies indicate that over half of the rape victims who file police reports are subjected to disturbing treatment by police officers (Patterson, D. 2011; Filipas & Ullman 2001; Monroe et al. 2005). Male officers tend to judge these situations more harshly when there is some type of illegal activity or substance abuse involved between the parties (El Sayed et al. 2022). Many victims of violence reported that the police were unfriendly and unhelpful (Nnawulezi, N. et al. 2022). Inappropriate responses by officers can trigger more victimization for those women who are already suffering from abuse (secondary victimization) and determine how these women will handle future instances (Goodman-Delahunty & Crehan 2016). However, increased experience in dealing with these types of situations can help officers better understand appropriate responses. (El Sayed et al. 2022). (Pereira Vieira et al. 2022)

Further, because Black and Latina women have negative impressions of law enforcement and are unlikely to trust them, they are much less likely to call them for help in cases of domestic abuse than white women (Duhaney, P. 2022; Messing et al. 2015). For example, reports suggest that Black women are more likely to be prosecuted because of IPV incidents (Bent-Goodley 2007). This could lead to the fear experienced by women in calling the police or reporting incidents of violence. Therefore, when Black and Latina women do contact the police, the abuse that they experience is usually much more severe and, in many cases, life-threatening (Campbell, D.W. et al. 2002; Messing et al. 2015). Much of the cause of these negative impressions is a result of unfair treatment that these women have experienced with law enforcement in the past, coupled with an overall lack of helpfulness (Duhaney, P. 2022; Messing et al. 2015). This unfair treatment includes a failure to offer help in these situations, demeaning comments about the incident or individuals, facetious attitudes towards the case, and a lack of trust in victims (Campbell, A.M. et al., 2020). Minority survivors' unfavorable interactions with law enforcement tend to prevent them from continuing to use the justice system as a formal source of support. (Harper, Grover, & Mages 2021)

Secondary victimization occurs throughout the victim's interactions with the criminal justice system, beginning with law enforcement (Parsons, J. & Bergin, T. 2010). In sexual assault cases, the victim's personality, demeanor, and credibility may play a crucial part in determining charges (Spohn, C. & Tellis, K. 2012). In many circumstances, there may be little physical evidence linking the defendant to the crime, and there are often no witnesses who can confirm the victim's account (Spohn, C. & Tellis, K. 2012). Therefore, the possibility of conviction primarily hinges on the victim's ability to explain what transpired and convince a judge or jury. Considering this, prosecutors base their assessments of "convictability" and, consequently, their charging decisions on their projections of how the victim's background, character, and behavior will be viewed and judged by other decision-makers, most notably potential jurors. (Kaiser, O'Neil, & Spohn 2017). This poses a severe difficulty for victims. When victims think that the criminal justice system employs unfair methods, it has a negative effect on their recovery by increasing the frequency and severity of PTSD symptoms (Wemmers 2013).

For the few cases involving women who have been the victim of violence that are prosecuted and result in a trial, the defense typically attempts to undermine the victim based on her behavior and actions and how they do not conform to those of a typical victim, whatever that may be (Larcombe 2002). This involves calling attention to any contradictions in her behavior, which may include her emotional response to the assault (Klippenstine & Schuller, 2012). As a result, a victim who responds inconsistently over time may be believed less than a victim who responds consistently, even if those behaviors are a result of trauma and can be explained (Klippenstine & Schuller, 2012))

It is important to note that because of the consistent re-victimization of IPV victims, a growing field of research suggests less criminalization of domestic violence in favor of a more balanced approach. Treating these systems as black and white, without any grey area (i.e., a person is either "guilty" or "not guilty" is going to be ineffective for women who want to explain their stories or receive some type of fair and just result (Walklate, Fitz-Gibbon, & McCulloch, J. 2018). These researchers argue that the U.S.'s current approach to domestic violence has led to a need for a more graduated response to IPV that does not intentionally harm the victims (Goodmark 2017). This issue is not primarily about criminal justice but instead an issue of health, economics, societal acceptance, and human rights (Goodmark 2018). However, no matter what approach this country takes, one group of women is clearly excluded from the conversation, especially related to issues of criminal justice.

BWS as a Defense in Court

For purposes of this section, it is important to consider the difference between types of defenses. An affirmative defense is one in which a defendant admits that they committed a crime but provides that they had a justifiable reason for doing so. Previously, these defenses were known as "justifiable" defense. While self-defense is an affirmative defense under current laws, BWS is not. Instead, it is presented as a psychological phenomenon used to explain why the use of self-defense is justifiable (Cornia 1997). To be able to explain BWS in court, the defense introduces an expert. However, before expert testimony on the BWS may be allowed in court, it must satisfy several legal conditions. As with all evidence, the testimony must meet the standard of "relevance" by helping to prove or disprove a material issue (Fla. Stat. 90.401). Additionally, any potential detrimental or prejudiced impacts must not outweigh the probative value of the testimony (Fla. Stat. 90.403). In addition to these criteria, expert testimony must also meet three further admission requirements. Although there is some variance in the courts' interpretations of each of these conditions, the following is the general thrust of the requirements: (1) The testimony is based upon sufficient facts or data; (2) The testimony is the product of reliable principles and methods; and (3) The witness has applied the principles and methods reliably to the facts of the case (Fla. Stat. 90.702).

Criticisms of BWS as a Legal Defense

There are many criticisms of BWS as a legal defense. The research surrounding BWS, and the court system is outdated. One clue comes from the fact that the reason is still referred to as BWS, whereas clinicians consider the term archaic (Friedman, Sorrentino, & Landess 2022). Robert Schopp et al. (1994) articulated the problems with BWS as a legal defense. First, although courts typically allow experts to testify about BWS in specific cases, the testimony is usually insufficient to consider it as a form of self-defense or as a clinical syndrome. Second, the testimony presented about BWS in court usually is not relevant to the self-defense standard, even to the case for which it is presented. Third, expert testimony focuses more on BWS, which is irrelevant in many cases, instead of addressing the specific details of the victim's relationship with her abuser. Fourth, many of these cases can be described sufficiently under customary self-defense laws (Kinports 2014). Finally, the courts have not produced a clear distinction between many legal concepts, including the difference between justification and excuse for crimes. Therefore, it is hard to develop a straightforward method to present BWS. (Schopp, R. F., Sturgis, B. J., & Sullivan, M., 1994)

Jurors require background information on the dynamics of domestic abuse to rationally evaluate the importance of the supplied evidence (De Sanctis, L.M. 1996). Evidence suggests that victims of IPV are most prejudiced in court when the finder of fact remains uneducated about BWS (Mechanic 2022; Lutz 2017). One study found that the introduction of BWS in court led female jurors to be more lenient, while it led male jurors to be harsher on the victim (Marshall, C. C. 2022). Since expert testimony on BWS is the only method to introduce domestic abuse in the court, it is usually used to explain psychological issues that determine the victim's credibility (Raeder, M.S. 1996). This means that currently, women have no other legal method for introducing evidence of prior abuse at the hands of her abuser, in court proceedings, outside of conceding that the woman has some type of psychological issues. However, in cases that do not involve issues of credibility, the testimony should be focused on describing the abusive relationship, not BWS (Raeder, M.S. 1996). Testimony presented by these experts in many cases has nothing to do with whether these women are suffering from BWS. However, it must be introduced because that is the only way to get into the cycle of abuse (Raeder, M.S. 1996). Due to the current court restrictions on the introduction of evidence, this flawed theory is the only way victims can present this testimony (Raeder, M. S. 1996).

BWS has been used by the judiciary to support the idea that women who have "acted up" should be pardoned by society. The problem with this way of thinking is that these women have not "acted up" at all. Instead, they have had a natural and justifiable reaction of defending themselves in response to a traumatic event. Therefore, these women do not need to be pardoned because their actions should not constitute a crime (Corina 1997). Although BWS testimony is intended to help jurors understand and apply a reasonableness standard to cases involving women accused of harming or murdering an abusive partner, some jurors may interpret the testimony as evidence of the psychological disorder of the female defendant (Mahoney 1991). They have concentrated on the "learned helplessness" portion of Lenore Walker's theory while ignoring its intricate details (Corina 1997). This viewpoint has adverse effects on all women in society by portraying them as irrational, flawed individuals who require special accommodations, which lowers the effectiveness of BWS in protecting women who kill (Ferraro 2017; Corina 1997).

Further, BWS categorizes women and assumes all women have similar reactions to trauma (Kohn, L.S. 2002). This creates a bias for fact finders in that it forces them to judge the victim's credibility on how well she conformed to traditional notions of how a battered woman is supposed to act (Mechanic 2022). When women do not respond within these given social norms, they are presumed to be dishonest and untrustworthy (Kohn 2002). Misconceptions work against these women, especially when they fail to report the incident to various agencies such as police, social workers, and healthcare providers (Kohn 2002). Jurors tend to rely on their own experiences to determine the reasonableness of a victim's actions, which can interfere with their ability to judge the victim fairly (Mechanic 2022).

This idea of how women behave poses a severe risk. BWS-based defenses promote a patriarchal view of society by stressing that battered women have "learned helplessness" (Ferraro 2017). This theory is based on the idea that because women are inferior to men, courts must make special provisions to address their deficiencies. Therefore, the defense puts out the theory that women are less capable of exercising reasonable self-control than men are, which exposes them to various interference kinds that men do not encounter.

This perspective is consistent with how women have historically been treated in the criminal justice system, which has routinely exonerated women who fit the traditional ideals of what a "victim" should look like, of criminal responsibility on the basis that their abilities are inferior to men's. This perspective, however, puts women at risk because it upholds the long-standing legal presumption that women should or must be submissive to men (Baker. K. K. 2005; Savage, J. 2006). (Coughlin 1994)

The "Why did she stay" Rhetoric

Whenever cases involve violence against women who have been in a relationship, the question of "why did she stay?" or "Couldn't she have left?" is always raised. Ignoring the many problematic stereotypes and ideologies surrounding these types of questions, research suggests that there are many valid reasons why women stay in abusive situations to the point where they snap, and violence becomes the only answer. In fact, there is a lot of research surrounding this phenomenon. Not surprisingly, research shows that men present higher levels of victim blaming than women, and IPV offenders showed higher levels of victim blaming than men from the general population (Martín-Fernández, et al. 2018).

The category of "battered woman" is difficult to understand because it is not a single, isolated event but instead a continuous cycle where women stay or return to abusive behavior (Walker 1979; Loseke and Cahill 1984; LaVoilette & Barnett 2013). Many have a tough time understanding why women return to abusive relationships because it violates the accepted principle that people act in their own best interest when they are allowed to do so (Dunn 2005).

One study found there are three themes for why women stay: (1) an abuser that threatens to increase the violence if she leaves (Mahoney 1994; Baddam 2017); (2) psychological factors, such as traumatic bonding, which is "the development of emotional attachments in battered women and other relationships of intermittent abuse (LaViolette & Barnett 2013 *citing* Dutton & Painter 1993) and situational factors. For example, women who leave may have been financially dependent, especially if they were unable (or not allowed) to work; therefore, leaving could result in homelessness (Tutty, L. M., et al. 2013; Angel 2014); and (3) the entrapment of these women between gender roles and patriarchy and the unsupportive social circles, coupled with financial dependence and housing insecurities that force them to stay in abusive relationships (Peled et al. 2000; Estrellado & Loh 2014). (Dunn 2005; Peled et al. 2000)

Further, these women may experience a sense of "learned helplessness," a phrasing first developed by Martin Seligman in the 1960s (Seligman & Maier 1967). Then, in the 1970s, Lenore Walker used this theory to apply to women who have been victims of abuse (Walker 1979). According to this theory, one of the elements experienced by battered women is that they have cognitive motivational impairments created by the abuse that they have suffered. This impairment prevents them from asking for assistance or information, which makes them feel out of control and convinces them there is nothing they can do to stop the abuse (Burgess-Proctor, A. 2012; Walker 1979). Some women who have been abused may even internalize the violence and begin to blame themselves, thinking they are to blame and deserving of punishment (Smart & Smart 1978 *cited by* Thapar-Björkert, S., & Morgan, K. J. 2010). This could be due to the significant cognitive and emotional trauma that impairs their ability to perceive the benefits or even possibilities of leaving the relationship (Ali & Naylor 2013).

Because of this learned helplessness, leaving an abusive relationship has been described as a process rather than as a single event (Enander, V., & Holmberg, C. 2008; Murray, C. E., Crowe, A., & Flasch, P. 2015). It is a process that begins at the cognitive level when women recognize that they are in an abusive relationship and are victims of abusive relationships (Crisostomo et al. 2012; Estrellado & Loh 2014). Studies have also revealed the circumstances and elements that led women to decide to end the cycle of abuse. Women leaving an abusive relationship have been found to be brought to this decision by an increase in the severity or frequency of the abuse (Estrellado & Loh, 2014; Sabina, C. & Tindale, R.S. 2008), the loss of hope that the relationship will improve, observing the detrimental impact of the abuse on the children and material resources (Varcoe, C. & Irwin, L.G. 2004; Moe 2009), or external pressures/advice from friends, family, and other professionals who provide support and alternative viewpoints (Estrellado & Loh, 2014;). The process of ending abuse is a lot more complicated than "just leaving." (Murray, C. E., Crowe, A., & Flasch, P. 2015)

The Erasure of Black Women

In reviewing the literature related to IPV victims, it seems that much of the literature specifically, although possibly unintentionally, relates directly to White women (Taft et al. 2009). Although BWS appears to be a defense applicable to all women, Black women must be evaluated separately because of their radically diverse circumstances (Lee, R.K. et al. 2002; Taft et al. 2009). However, the literature is limited in involving Black and other non-majority women (Lee, R. K. et al. 2002; Taft et al. 2009). Many studies either do not include a statistically considerable number of women of color in their sample size or do not use statistical techniques to differentiate between the ethnic groups (Stockman, J. K., et al. 2015). Even when studies do include women of color, research results addressing racial differences are either inconclusive or do not apply to minority women in the same ways they apply to White women (Cho 2012). This deficiency creates a significant gap in the literature because studies show Black women are at an increased risk for severe IPV (West 2021; Kelly et al. 2020; St. Vil, N.M. 2017; Lacey et al. 2016;). However, this invisibility of Black women in the literature is consistent with their treatment throughout history.

Since the inception of this country, Black women have been simply forgotten about, and when they are not forgotten, they still are not seen as credible. These issues are created due to Black women's intersectional identity as both women and people of color within discourses and cause their interests and experiences to be frequently marginalized within both categories (Crenshaw 2013). In examining this research, we can see how Black women have been victimized and later blamed for defending themselves after becoming victims of sexual violence (Harper, Grover, & Mages 2021). There were many ways African American women were erased during the mid-20th century when they attempted to use self-defense. For example, many times during the Jim Crow era, when women would defend themselves, it would be a direct result of suffering from abuse that had been left unpunished however, that abuse was often left out of the narrative (Jones, L.E. 2018). These situations would be labeled as a crime committed by the Black woman as opposed to self-defense (Jones, L.E. 2018). Further, the media attempted to reframe the issues of domestic violence issues of stereotypes, and segregation so they did not become public issues (Ponton, D. 2018).

However, in more recent times, many of the resistances to white supremacy were brought on by Black women. A fitting example of this is the civil rights movement, which was perpetuated by Black women who refused to be "swept under the rug" after being the victim of sexual violence. Still, in looking back through history, it seems like all the work done by these women has been diminished, and their resistance to sexual violence has been ignored to make space for narratives of Black men or white women in the Civil Rights and Women's Movements. (McGuire 2011).

These historical issues create present-day problems for Black women as it relates to IPV because there are many differences between Black women and those of other descent in how they respond to IPV, some of which can be attributed to their historical treatment and subsequent adaptation. For example, Black women are less likely than women of other ethnic backgrounds to try to get help for IPV from traditional agencies because of inherent racism in the system and fears of stigmas (Kelly et al. 2020; Monterrosa 2021; Anyikwa 2015). Instead, many seek help from religion, gain employment or education to become financially independent, leave, or turn to family and friends (St. Vil et al. 2017). Black women may also blame themselves for abuse and, in turn, attempt suicide, or think about attempting suicide often. (Sigurvinsdottir et al. 2020). Black women are also more likely to fight back against their abuser, which could then escalate the violence and cause them to be arrested as a perpetrator instead of a victim (St. Vil et al. 2017; West 2007). These unique coping mechanisms illustrate the increasing need for focused research involving this marginalized group.

Along the same lines, the "sexual abuse to prison pipeline" points out how many times women who have been the victim of sexual assault become criminalized after they have been victimized (Henderson 2020). An example of this can be seen with human trafficking victims who are arrested for prostitution. Further, women of color are disproportionately affected by these criminal justice practices (Starr 2015). Therefore, not only are these women not taken seriously as victims of violence, but they are also then criminalized as victims.

Recent research suggests there is a level of *toxic Black femininity*, which is "the internalized and dominant message that, as a Black woman, one must be rigidly strong, hypersexual, and primary caregiver to all, before acknowledging or taking care of one's own needs and desires" (Kelly et al. 2020, pp. 55) This becomes relevant in cases of IPV because Black women may fail to report incidents of IPV or receive needed assistance because of their need to maintain an image of a healthy environment for their children. Further, stereotypes of becoming a single mother become increasingly relevant during attempts to leave the abuser. Studies show many Black women fear being forced to remain single due to a lack in the availability of Black men (West 2007). (Kelly et al. 2020)

Another issue that causes the invisibility of Black women after they have been the victim of IPV is a lack of resources at all levels (Taft et al. 2009). As stated earlier, Black women are more at risk for severe IPV than White or Hispanic women, yet, they have limited access to services necessary to be able to cope with these situations (Kelly et al. 2020). The intersection of poverty and anti-Black racism makes help-seeking behaviors ineffective, if not impossible (Haynes-Thoby, L. 2019). Much of the recent literature surrounding Black women explores this dilemma.

It is essential to discuss Black women who live at the intersection of poverty and violence because they have an extra set of challenges in receiving help for these situations. Separately but equally, issues surrounding poverty and those surrounding IPV affect the physical and mental health of the women forced to endure these problems (Goodman. L.A. et al. 2015) then Black women are forced to deal with an entirely separate group of the issues, as stated above (Gillum 2019).

Poverty has been identified as a critical risk factor in IPV, no matter what race the couples are (WHO 2012; Cunradi, C. B. 2000; Ahmadabadi, Z. et al. 2020). Neighborhoods with more problems, usually characteristic of impoverished areas, can create stressors in which IPV is more likely to occur (Kirst, M. et al. 2015). Additionally, Black women report high IPV experiences on a consistent basis (Alexander, K.A. et al. 2021; Basile, K.C. et al. 2011). As stated earlier, Black women are less likely to seek help from formal organizations as the victim of IPV, but research also shows that poverty may lead victims without resources to seek help due to being unaware of the resources, distrusting the resources, being financially dependent on the abuser, or simply resource unavailability (Sabri, B. et al. 2015; Kennedy et al. 2012; Alexander, K.A. 2021) Ultimately, the research is clear that Black women living in poverty are at an increased likelihood of experiencing IPV with a decreased chance of being able to receive the services necessary to combat the mental and physical impacts of this intersection. Yet, as this dissertation will demonstrate, Black women are particularly vulnerable under previous and current laws established in this country.

SYG

SYG laws are the most recent iteration of self-defense laws in the United States. They provide that individuals do not have to retreat from dangerous situations and can "stand their ground" when they are in fear of great bodily harm or death. The idea behind them is that law-abiding citizens should not have to run from "bad guys" and should be able to defend themselves without fear of retribution from the justice system. While not all states have these laws, the number is growing by the day. As of November 2022, only three states and the Federal system have no form of SYG laws (*See* Appendix A). However, although the laws are famous within specific ideological camps in the U.S., they are not necessarily the best way to protect people who have been victims of violence. We see a clear gap in the protection provided to women who have been the victim of repeat violence and choose to retaliate after the danger has subsided. Although there has been some research on the issues, the law in this area is continuously evolving, which leaves a lot of room for improvement in the literature and changes to the law.

Overview

When the SYG law was initially enacted in Florida, it did not raise many questions or spark national attention (Iyler 2022). There was not much interest in the subject, so the related literature was scarce. However, in 2012 the case of *State of Florida v. George Zimmerman* arose. This case brought the SYG laws in Florida to the forefront nationally and had many researchers questioning its effects. The jury returned a "not guilty" verdict based on standing his ground as an affirmative defense. After being instructed on this law, many took it as a wake-up call to the dangerous potential of the law. Since then, there has been a lot of research conducted on the rules, even though much of it has not actually been turned into reading materials.

One of the leading examinations of the SYG laws was done by Caroline Light in a book entitled *Stand your ground: A History of America's Love Affair with Lethal Self Defense*. In this book, Light uses a historical perspective to understand the evolution of the self-defense laws in the

United States that have resulted in the SYG laws. The book examines explicitly self-defense as it evolved in Florida, mainly because it was written shortly after the verdict in the famous *State v. George Zimmerman* case to understand how it happened and why it should not have been surprising. The ultimate thesis of the book is that self-defense laws have always worked disproportionately against minorities (Light 2017).

One study examined the homicide rates in Florida before and after the implementation of SYG laws and found that homicides were decreasing before SYG was implemented; however, after the implementation, there was a sudden and consistent increase in the rates. The study examined states that had not implemented the law and did not find any increase in homicide rates during the same time. Further, in Florida, gun violence related to suicide also showed no change in rates. (Humphreys, Gasparrini, & Wiebe 2017)

Along the same lines, research has shown that SYG laws do not reduce crimes, but instead, they either have no effect or increase crime rates (Guis 2016). Proponents of SYG laws would argue that these laws deal with the aftereffects of crimes by reducing barriers to exercising self-defense (Editorial Board 2022). SYG did not get passed as an appeal to the legislature by advocating for more lenient laws against violence, but instead, to allow "law-abiding citizens" (who are usually White) to protect themselves from "criminals" (who are generally Black and Brown), an argument that is still maintained today (Coker 2014; Megale 2014). However, this study also found that states that have enacted SYG laws have higher crime rates for some crimes and no effect for others; however, these laws have not been shown to lower crime rates (Guis 2016; McClellan, C. 2017; Everytown for Gun Safety 2019). The fact of the matter is that certain groups of people benefit from these laws while others do not.

Another troubling finding related to SYG laws is that under the SYG law when Whites shooters have a Black victim and claim self-defense, it is found to be justified at a much higher rate when compared to Black shooters with White victims. However, in non-SYG states, although the rates were still disproportionate, the justification of White shooters with Black victims was much lower, while Black shooters with White victims remained the same. Further, White on-Black homicides are justified more than three times more than White on White homicides. (Roman 2016)

The American Bar Association (ABA) compiled a report in 2015 including all the prior mentioned studies and examining the SYG laws independently. The ABA's task force found that the SYG laws resulted in the unpredictable, disproportionate treatment of defendants to the disadvantage of minorities. Further, the task force found that the public was sufficiently protected before SYG. Additionally, they discovered that SYG did result in increased homicide rates. Finally, they found that the victims of crimes suffered because of SYG laws. Based on these conclusions, they found that the self-defense laws should be repealed (Laws 2015).

SYG laws have developed in a way that does not protect women from violence. The rules do not consider the various responses women have after being victims of violence. Further, it is essential to point out that though we have seen an evolution in both self-defense laws outside of the home as well as with castle doctrine laws, we have not seen a convergence of the two. Many states do not have regulations in place to account for victims and aggressors that live in the same home, causing several courts to still struggle in these situations (Messerschmidt 2016). In many cases, we see a higher burden placed on victims of domestic violence who live together, requiring them to retreat further than they can, as opposed to individuals who are strangers (Messerschmidt 2016). In many of these cases, SYG laws are providing a space for these men to attack strangers in public but also attack their wives in the privacy of their own homes, who are forced to rely on the un-equal defense of BWS and beg for the Court's mercy (Franks 2013).

SYG and BWS (IPV)

Although research in SYG as it relates to BWS and IPV is relatively new, some studies have examined the topic. Most of these articles suggest the same conclusions that the above research shows, that SYG does not protect women who have been the victim of violence (Crisafi 2016). We can see from these effects that these laws were not created for women because "(I)f SYG reforms were in fact driven by concerns for women's vulnerability, the paradigmatic rape scenario would have been one that most women are likely to face: the rape by someone the victim knows and trusts, not the stranger imagined in supporters' narratives." (Franks 2013, pp. 1109). It has become abundantly clear that the SYG laws reinforce already existing societal gender roles by honoring the "True Man" doctrine through SYG laws while leaving women with the "helpless woman begging for forgiveness from mental deficiencies of BWS defenses (Keegan 2013).

Research suggests that there are more burdens placed on victims of IPV in the criminal justice system than there are protections for them (Crisafi 2016). For example, current SYG laws do not allow women to protect themselves using deadly force unless they have a protective order against the assailant; and if the woman does have a protective order, the law does not clearly state that the woman does have a presumption of reasonableness either, just, at best, that they might. (Franks 2013). This is ludicrous given that there is a presumption of fear when a stranger enters their home, but when a known abuser does the same, there is no presumption (Fla. Stat. 776.013(4)).

SYG laws were based upon masculine assumptions and beliefs in threats from dangerous strangers. Since most women's self-defensive behavior is against men they know – not threatening strangers – and they do not kill their abusers when the danger is imminent (opting instead to use force when abusers are sleeping or otherwise not posing an immediate threat), SYG or traditional self-defense laws provide them no legal protection (Gillis 2020; Walker 2009; Linklaters LLP 2016). Therefore, the problem with SYG laws is that they were not designed with IPV victims in mind. Consequently, it is evident that there is a limited understanding of how these scenarios work and how to include requirements such as "reasonable" and "imminent" disadvantaged victims (Cristafi 2016). The reasonableness standard cannot be objective because judges and jurors are biased. These biases include things such as patriarchy, stereotypes, misunderstandings of IPV, and victim blaming. All these issues work to disadvantage victims (Jackson 2015).

Further, SYG laws seem to be even worse for victims who are also Black women. The problem for these women is that even for Black woman experiencing abuse, there is a false societal perception that these laws provide all women an affirmative defense. This encourages abuse victims to use lethal force to defend themselves because they feel the laws protect them. However, our societal norms fail to consider that women of color are not treated the same in the criminal justice system, despite being the most vulnerable to abuse. Now, the laws are further marginalizing these women instead of keeping them safe due to the inherent biases present in the criminal justice system. (Ijoma, S. 2018)

There was a solution proposed in these ideas. Instead of placing such high burdens on victims of IPV, we could instead grant immunity to people who defend themselves in their own homes, even against co-inhabitants (Jackson 2015). This could be accomplished by presuming women who have been the victim of domestic abuse were, in fact, defending themselves (Jackson 2015). While this paper does not explore this potential solution further, it is clear that a problem exists that requires a solution.

Gaps in the Literature

In reviewing the literature related to SYG laws and IPV, a few gaps have become known. This area of the law is relatively new and continuously evolving, which makes it hard for researchers to keep up. The central argument that this research will attempt to make is that SYG laws, and self-defense laws in general, were never designed to protect women. In fact, laws that protect women and the issues related to women have evolved separately from those that are designed to save men (Crisafi 2016). The rules that protect women are continuously framed as a mental health illness as opposed to a justifiable excuse under the law. While the laws that protect men are constantly expanding and include more cases, the rules involving women are constantly under attack and being constricted. This dissertation will show why in a more novel way by not only studying individual circumstances and what happened throughout the court process, including case studies but also including interviews from actual practitioners in the field, a method that is seldom used in these research studies.

After a thorough review of the literature, it is also clear that there have been few studies done on the impact of intersectionality on self-defense laws. For example, there are studies that exist on women and self-defense laws, there are studies that exist on Black people and self-defense laws, and there are, to a smaller extent, studies on women and self-defense laws. However, very few, if any, studies explore the relationship between Black, poor women, and self-defense laws. Therefore, future research should examine these factors.

The next chapter will demonstrate the significance of existing research along with the strengths and weaknesses of Florida's SYG laws through an in-depth overview of the history of self–defense throughout the state to show that current SYG laws are insufficient to support women who have been the victim of physical or sexual violence and decide to fight back.

Chapter Two: Legal Analysis

One of the most critical parts of this dissertation is to make sure that we look at specific Florida cases to determine how SYG laws are being applied in practice. Further, what have been the results of the cases, and are there any differences between how issues are being handled, both over time and between men and women? Therefore, this Chapter will discuss specific cases that have occurred in Florida throughout recent history. The data contained in this Chapter shows us that SYG laws are in full effect and functioning as they were intended, providing the necessary protection for men, specifically White men. However, women are not receiving the same result.

This Chapter provides additional support for the proposition that SYG laws are rooted in racist, patriarchal ideologies that have led to the unequal treatment of women in the criminal justice system. This Chapter contributes to the literature by providing a road map through Florida cases and statutes that have been influential in the development of SYG laws as we know them today. This Chapter compares the legislative and judicial history of self-defense for women, beginning with the castle doctrine and evolving into the BWS defense, and compares it to the evolution of SYG laws. The takeaway is that throughout the different iterations of self-defense laws that have now developed into SYG laws, those that relate to women who have been the victim of physical violence, especially within their home, have evolved separately and unequally from self-defense laws that protect men, which then systematically disadvantages these women, and many times leaves them unprotected under the law.

A History of SYG laws in the United States

The history of self-defense in the United States can be traced all the way back to English common law in the 1600s. *Semayne's case*, 5 Co Rep 91 a (1604), was decided on January 1, 1604, and reported by Sir Edward Coke of England. This case was about whether the Sherriff had a right to enter Semayne's home, which is not related to self-defense. However, the Court, according to Sir Coke, stated, "the house of everyone is to him as his castle and fortress, as well for his defence (sp.) against injury and violence as for his repose." This famous quote became known as the "Castle Doctrine," which stands for the notion that a man has the right to defend himself in his home. Since this case, the castle doctrine has been well settled as commonplace within the United States. All states and the federal government have adopted some form of legislation confirming this principle.

The early implementation of the Castle Doctrine was a foreshadowing of where self-defense laws would be in the 21st century as we now move away from the duty to retreat. However, this doctrine only applies to individuals while in their homes and is only a tiny piece of current SYG laws related to the defense of oneself or others. Therefore, it is essential to keep looking at the self-defense laws to see how we developed our rules to present-day legislation.

From *Semayne's case,* the following central common law principle that we can see remnants from is located within Blackstone's Commentaries. William Blackstone was an English lawyer that lived in the 1700s. He became one of the first professors of English law, and it was this role that allowed him to write commentaries on English Law. These commentaries provide a complete overview of English law. These books, published in 1770, 1773, 1774, 1775, and 1778, and in a posthumous edition in 1783, have been regarded as one of the most accurate ways to understand English law of the 1700s (Jack Miller Center 2018). Blackstone's commentaries were commonly cited in many early cases decided in the United States and remain a backbone of much of American law. Blackstone is still used by many legal scholars when attempting to navigate through complex legal issues that may be better understood in a historical context.

In reviewing these commentaries, Blackstone specifically discusses self-defense in his chapter on homicide. Blackstone describes two types of justified homicide, *per infortunium* (misadventure) or *se defendeo* (self-preservation). *Se defendeo* is the means that would be most closely related to self-defense today. In describing this type of killing, Blackstone states that this type of homicide is justifiable, not excusable. Excusable killings would be those that are done in the lawful execution of a legal duty, such as an execution pursuant to a lawful sentence or a police officer killing an assailant in the line of duty (Blackstone 1966).

In describing *per infortunium*, Blackstone states that it is an act that is done when there are "no other means of escape from the perpetrator" (Blackstone 1966, p. 184). Specifically, Blackstone explains that "the law sets so high a value upon the life of a man that it always intends some misbehavior in the person who takes it away, unless by the command or express permission of the law" (Blackstone 1966, p. 184)." Further, he states that it is not a means of attacking someone and, therefore, should only be exercised in extreme circumstances (Blackstone 1966).

In looking at this explanation of self-defense by Blackstone, it leaves many questions. The biggest of those questions is how we evolved from using self-defense in extreme circumstances to using self-defense whenever it could be justified. This is precisely contrary to the teachings of Blackstone. Therefore, we must continue to examine the history of self-defense to understand this shift.

In continuing to look throughout history, there were a lot of cases throughout the late 1800s, all over the United States, that led the Supreme Court to determine that there was no duty to retreat.

For example, the phrase "stand your ground" first appeared in case law in *Beard v. United States, 158 U.S. 550* (1895). Beard was a white farmer from Arkansas whose nephews came to visit him with the intention of stealing a cow. The Court specifically mentioned that his nephews had previously made threats that Beard knew about, to the effect that they would either get the cow or kill Beard in the attempt. Beard armed himself and went out to confront his nephews. The lower court instructed the jury that because Beard did this, he forfeited his right to self-defense and that, furthermore, he was required to retreat if he could do so safely. Beard, as Justice Harlan wrote for a unanimous Supreme Court, "was entitled to stand his ground and meet any attack made upon him with a deadly weapon in such way and with such force as, under all the circumstances, he at the moment, honestly believed, and had reasonable grounds to believe, were necessary to save his own life or protect himself from great bodily injury" (*Id.* at 564).

This case is an even greater extension of the law than what we have today. However, since it occurred on private property, it could have been distinguished from other self-defense cases as an extension of the castle doctrine. Therefore, it is important to continue throughout history to see how the Supreme Court would rule in patients that did not apply to private property. Was this just an extension of the castle doctrine?

From *Beard*, we can then look to *Brown v. United States, 256 U.S. 335* (1921). The facts of this case begin with a story of trouble and tension between Brown and Hermis. There was evidence that Hermis had assaulted Brown with a knife on two separate occasions, and during the last altercation, he had even stated that the next time one of them would "go off in a black box" (*Id.* at 342). On the day in question, Brown was superintending excavation work, and because of the previous threats made by Hermis, Brown had taken a pistol with him to work and was carrying it in his coat. Hermis came up to the site with another individual with a cart to be loaded. Brown told him that certain parts of the land were not to be removed, and according to Brown, this caused

Hermis to come toward him with a knife. Brown left and got his pistol from his coat, which was

about twenty-five feet away. As Hermis was coming at him with the knife, Brown fired four shots

and killed him.

Based on these facts, the trial judge instructed the jury, among other things, that "it is

necessary to remember, in considering the question of self-defense, that the party assaulted is

always under the obligation to retreat so long as retreat is open to him, provided that he can do so

without subjecting himself to the danger of death or great bodily harm." (*Id.*at 342). This was in

line with Blackstone's standard law definition of self-defense in his commentaries. However,

Justice Holmes, delivering the opinion of the Supreme Court, stated

> Detached reflection cannot be demanded in the presence of an uplifted knife. Therefore, in
> this Court at least, it is not a condition of immunity that one in that situation should pause
> to consider whether a reasonable man might not think it possible to fly with safety or to
> disable his assailant, rather than to kill him (*Id.* at 343).
>
> The opinions of the Court in these two cases seem to be precisely in line with the self-

defense laws we see today, while the lower courts were more in line with Blackstone's notion.

Therefore, although it seems like the policymakers have created an entirely new concept in their

policymaking decisions related to self-defense, they may just be creating laws to support the

rulings made by the Supreme Court. If the legislature makes laws and the Supreme Court continues

to overturn the laws within their orders, eventually, the legislature will change the way policies

are written, which seems to be what may have happened in these cases.

The Castle Doctrine

As mentioned earlier, the United States has consistently recognized a man's interest in

protecting his home and given deference to that interest. For example, the Supreme Court of the

United States recognized the long-standing Castle Doctrine and a man's ability to *stand his ground* in defense of his home and property in *Beard v. United States,* 158 So. 550 (1985). The language, in this opinion, uses masculine pronouns, and it is not a coincidence. In 1985 women had just gained rights to own property outside of their husbands 40 years ago through the married women's property act, which was passed in Florida in 1846 (Clark 2010). Although it was not explicitly stated in the laws, the biases against women were still present.

Florida cases first mention the Castle Doctrine in *Wilson v. State,* 11 So. 556 (1892). This case does not explicitly state that a man does not have a duty to retreat but instead states that he should "meet the assailant at the threshold and use the amount of force that is necessary for his and their (his family's) protection" *Id.* at 558. We can see from this language that the laws which come later stem from this premise. The problem with this is that it assumes that the man is responsible for defending his family and that the other members of the family are helpless. It does not consider that the man could be the aggressor, and one of the other members of the family might need to protect themselves from him. We can see the problems that follow with SYG laws based on these sexist premises.

The next time we see SYG language clarified in Florida law is in *Pell v. State* 122 So. 116 (1929). In this case, the victim was a police officer who was executing a search warrant on the Defendant's home. That warrant was later found to be illegal, but the officer did not know that at the time of execution. The Defendant and his brother got into an altercation with the police officer, and the officer was killed during the struggle. The Supreme Court held that although the duty to retreat applies, "a man violently assaulted in his own house or on his premises near his house is not obliged to retreat but may stand his ground and use such force as may appear to him as a cautious and prudent man to be necessary to save his life or to save himself from great bodily harm." *Id.* This language eerily mirrors the language that we will see in future statutes, both in

Florida and elsewhere. However, it is again important to note that this language uses masculine pronouns, arguably because, during its inception, laws providing for self-defense were specifically designed for men only.

Another time we see laws that reference standing your ground occurs in *Hedges v. State* 172 So.2d 874 (1965), a case that contradicts the notion that these laws were not intended for women who have been the victim of sexual or other types of physical violence. The facts showed that Ms. Hedges' male companion attacked her in her home after she invited him over. She killed him during the attack. One of the issues on appeal was whether Ms. Hedges had a duty to retreat when being attacked in her own home by someone she invited over. The State argued that because Ms. Hedges invited the man into her home, she had a duty to retreat. However, the Court relied on *Pell* to find that the obligation to withdraw did not apply to Ms. Hedges. While this case could be used to support the proposition that even though the laws use masculine pronouns, they provide equal justification for women, this case must be looked at in more depth. *Id.*

Hedges was decided by the Supreme Court in 1965, but before it got there, it originated from the Second District Court of Appeals in 1964. The State's argument for differentiating this case from *Pell* was that *Pell* involved an intruder, but *Hedges* did not. However, in 1958, *Harris v. State,* 104 So.2d 739 (Fla. Dist. Ct. App. 1958) was also decided by the Second District Court of Appeals, a decision that should have been binding on the rulings in *Hedges.* In that case, the Defendant killed an invited guest at his home after the guest got into an altercation with Mr. Harris' daughter. The Court held that

> The law of self-defense requires everyone to avoid killing when possible and to retreat, if necessary, and consistent with his own safety before taking life; but when a person is in his own home, and he or members of his family are assaulted or placed in apparent imminent danger of significant personal injury, he has right to stand his ground and meet force with force, even to extent of taking life, if he actually believes, and circumstances and surrounding conditions are such

that a reasonably cautious prudent person would think, danger of death or significant personal injury to be imminent at hands of assailant. *Id.* at 743.

After knowing that in 1958 the *Harris* decision found that a person does not have a duty to retreat in their own home when "faced with imminent danger of great personal injury" *Id.* was binding on the Court in Hedges, which was initially decided in 1964; we must ask ourselves why Ms. Hedges was even sitting in the defendant's chair.

To continue this line of cases, we next look at *Watkins v. State,* 197 So. 2d 312 (Fla. 4th Dist. Ct. App. 1967). Mrs. Watkins' husband came home after a night of drinking, and the two had an argument. Mr. Watkins reached into his pocket where he usually kept a pocketknife. When she saw this, she shot and killed him. She testified that in the past, he had stabbed her with the knife under similar circumstances after a night of drinking, and on multiple occasions, he had also threatened to shoot her with his pistol. The Court relied on *Pell* and found that Ms. Watkins did not have a duty to retreat when in her own home. This case is more compelling than *Hedges* for the argument that the laws were being equally applied to women because now we have them involved in the Fourth District, which was not required to follow the Court in *Pell.*

This line of reasoning continues in *Stevenson v. State,* 285 So. 2d 61 (Fla. 4th Dist. Ct. App. 1973). In this case, the Fourth District used the same reasoning in *Watkins* to find that even though Ms. Stevenson and her husband were co-occupants, she did not have a duty to retreat when she was being actively attacked. *Id.* However, the perplexing thing about this case is that, like *Hedges*, there was already a previous finding by the same Court under the same facts that held that co-occupants did not have a duty to retreat, so why was Ms. Stevenson sitting in the Defendant's chair?

Limitations on the Castle Doctrine

While Florida experienced an extended period of expansion of laws allowing Defendants to stand their ground under the castle doctrine, towards the end of the 1970s, we saw a period of recission from these principles in some significant ways. These instances provide the few times Florida's Supreme Court has placed any limits on the castle doctrine. By placing limits on the defenses available to individuals who live in the same household, the Court is setting up the major uphill battle that women have consistently faced in getting access to the criminal justice system as a victim of IPV. The prevailing view became that when two people are both invited members of a household or live in that household, the standard for asserting self-defense is heightened.

In 1976, the case of Ann Marie Conner started to limit rights under the castle doctrine. Not much is known of Ms. Conner other than she was living with her son, who had some type of mental illness. There is no mention of whether she was living with a man as well, but it is assumed she did not. Annie Mae Conner was tried and convicted of killing her "mentally defective" son, who lived with her. *Conner v. State,* 361 So. 2d 774, 775 (Fla. Dist. Ct. App. 1978).

Ms. Conner maintained that she did not mean to shoot her son and did so only after he attacked her, while the prosecution argued that Ms. Conner's son was trying to apologize to her when she shot him and therefore was not a threat. *Id.* It is undisputed that the law at that time was that

One unlawfully attacked in his own home or on his own premises has no duty to retreat and may lawfully stand his ground and meet force with force, including deadly force, if necessary to prevent imminent death or great bodily harm to himself or another or to prevent the commission of a forcible felony. *Id.*

However, the Court refused to instruct on the defense of home because "both parties, according to the evidence, legally lived in the home, and the court would rule (it) to be bad law to allow either party to stand and not retreat." *Id.* The appellate court agreed with this decision and even stated that they were receding from their previous expansion of the castle doctrine when both parties were legally entitled to be in the home. *Id.* at 776.

It is important to note that *Conner* was decided by the same Court that decided both *Watkins* and *Stevenson,* yet *Conner* was decided in the opposite way less than ten years later. In theory, Ms. Conner should not have been a defendant because the law was already decided, yet she was, and the Court held an opinion contrary to its own prior rulings. Even if the individuals on the Court changed, the precedent to follow should have already been set. Yet, that was not the case, and it led to a continued uphill battle for women after that.

A few years later, the Supreme Court continued to apply the logic of *Conner* when faced with the case of Elsie Bobbit. Mrs. Bobbit was a white female who shot and killed her husband in Duval County on July 1, 1977, after he attacked her. There is no evidence that he did anything to provoke the attack, but there was evidence that Mr. Bobbit had been drinking and was drunk. He died from a single bullet wound to the chest. The evidence showed that Mr. Bobbit routinely beat Mrs. Bobbit and their children, and he was heard by neighbors threatening Mrs. Bobbit on the night of the incident. The neighbor called the police, but they did not get there until after the shooting had occurred. Mrs. Bobbit had not fired a gun prior to that night, and when the police arrived, she had a broken cheekbone consistent with being punched. *State v. Bobbit*, 389 So.2d 1094 (Fla. App. 1 Dist. 1980).

The Supreme Court extended the same logic to Ms. Bobbit's case as it had done in *Conner* and found:

> We hold that the privilege not to retreat, premised on the maxim that every man's home is his castle which he is entitled to protect from invasion, does not apply here where both Bobbitt and her husband had equal rights to be in the "castle" and neither had the legal right to eject the other. As Judge Letts pointed out in *Conner,* this holding does not leave an occupant of a home defenseless against the attacks of another legal co-occupant of the premises since "a person placed in imminent danger of death or great bodily harm to

himself by the wrongful attack of another has no duty to retreat if to do so would increase his own threat of death or significant physical injury. *Id.* at 726.

This case is perplexing because the testimony established that Mrs. Bobbit, like Ms. Conner, was in imminent danger of great bodily harm from her husband based on the injuries sustained and the history of violence, yet the Court still found that she had a duty to retreat before defending herself.

Re-Expansion of the Castle Doctrine

The law established in *Conner* remained in effect until the 1990s. It was then that *Weiand v. State,* 732 So. 2d 1044, 1048–49 (Fla. 1999), was decided. During this time, BWS, which will be discussed later, had been argued successfully in many other states and was becoming increasingly prevalent. This is important because it had some impact on the way this case was decided. That aspect will be discussed later; however, one key piece of this case addressed the castle doctrine, and it is essential to mention it here.

Kathleen Weiand was charged with first-degree murder for the 1994 shooting death of her husband, Todd Weiand. Mrs. Weiand shot her husband during an argument in their apartment where they were living with their seven-week-old daughter. At trial, Weiand claimed self-defense. Like Mrs. Bobbitt, Mrs. Weiand testified that her husband beat and choked her throughout their three-year relationship and threatened more violence if she left him. Two experts, including Dr. Lenore Walker, testified that Mrs. Weiand was suffering from BWS and that she shot her husband because she believed he was going to seriously hurt or kill her. *Id.*

The Supreme Court decided to rescind their prior rulings in both *Conner* and *Bobbit* and found that a person does not have to retreat in their own home from a co-occupant if they are in fear of great bodily harm or death, but if the person must use deadly force in self-defense, there is a limited duty to retreat. *Id.* at 1058. In other words, a person does not have to withdraw when using non-deadly force, but they should make some effort to retreat before using deadly force. This holding then became the prevailing standard in Florida.

In ruling this way, the Court acknowledged that they were departing from the ruling in *Bobbit* and gave four reasons for doing so. The first reason the court gave is that the *Bobbitt* decision was "grounded upon the sanctity of property and possessory rights, rather than the sanctity of human life." They call this an "illogical distinction" that affords more protection to a woman who kills her boyfriend who comes over for the night than to a woman whose husband batters her. *Id.* at. 1052.

Second, the Court decided to overrule *Bobbitt* because of its implications for victims of domestic violence. The court's concern was that imposing a duty to retreat from the home would adversely impact victims of domestic violence. The court cited a Florida Governor's Task Force on Domestic Violence report that states, "forty-five percent of the murders of women were generated by the man's rage over the actual or impending estrangement from his partner." *Id.* The states that are retaining a duty to retreat from the home handicaps women and wives from defending themselves against an aggressive spouse. *Id.* at. 1052- 1054.

The Court's third concern was that a jury instruction on duty to retreat would reinforce, legitimize, and strengthen myths and stereotypes about domestic violence. One of the most pervasive myths surrounding domestic violence is that women may leave an abusive situation whenever they want. *Id.* at 1054. The Court acknowledged this myth and attempted to combat it in this ruling.

The Court's final reason to overrule *Bobbit* and apply the castle doctrine to domestic abuse situations is based on "The Evolution of Public Policy" since *Bobbit* was decided in 1982. The court provided a lot of examples of how the law had evolved since the decision in *Bobbit,* thereby supporting the notion that the law should continue to grow as well. *Id.* at 1054 - 1056. All these reasons support the idea that the courts do not function in a vacuum, and many times when these decisions are made, they are based on prevailing public opinion and standards at that time, whether that works in a positive way or negative way. This is critical for understanding where the law has evolved since this case into SYG.

SYG Laws

In 2005, Florida enacted the first SYG statute in the country. These laws came as a direct result of the case law language from the previous century that provided individuals did not have a duty to retreat when in their homes. The preamble to the 2005 law states that citizens "have a right to expect to remain unmolested in their homes and vehicles, and no person or victim of a crime should be required to surrender his personal safety to a criminal, nor should a person or victim be required to needlessly retreat in the face of an intrusion or attack." Preamble for Senate Bill No. 436.

These laws are found in Florida Statute Chapter 776, where the prior self-defense laws were located. The central provision that makes the law "SYG" is the language providing that Defendants do not have a duty to retreat and can instead stand their ground in places where they have a lawful right to be, not just the home. Additionally, the law stated that individuals who are standing their ground are immune from both civil and criminal liability and could sue agencies for wrongfully arresting them. One of the other significant portions of the law was the provision allowing a presumption of fear for individuals defending their homes, making it even harder to prove charges against individuals who use force while protecting their property. The biggest weakness for women who have been the victim of sexual and physical violence is that the provision that contains the presumption of fear does not apply to individuals who have the legal right to be in the home, in many ways reverting to the holding in *Bobbit*, despite the detailed ruling in *Weiand* just a few years earlier. Therefore, scenarios in which women kill their abusive partners or spouse do not benefit from the provision.

In 2007, the Supreme Court had to address whether the SYG law would apply to cases in which Defendants were convicted of not retreating prior to this statute enacted in 2005. This issue was discussed in *Robert Lee Smiley* v. State, 966 So. 2d 330 (Fla. 2007). Robert Smiley was charged with first-degree premeditated murder that occurred on November 6, 2004. Mr. Smiley shot the victim, who was an occupant of Mr. Smiley's cab. Mr. Smiley claimed self-defense but was convicted after the jury was told he had a duty to retreat. The Supreme Court of Florida found that the SYG statute did not apply retroactively. *Smiley v. State,* 966 So. 2d 330 (Fla. 2007)

Expanding SYG: Immunity Hearings

From the inception of SYG laws, what we have seen has been a continuous expansion in a variety of ways, with little to no added limitations. This is important because when we look at these expansions, none of them directly benefit women who have been the victim of sexual or other physical violence and have already been limited in their households by not being afforded the benefit of a presumption of fear. These laws use similar language to that used in the late 1800s when women were afforded no rights. By reverting to this language, we have adopted the same principles and ideas from those times that afford little to no protection for women.

In 2006, Clarence Dennis was charged with the attempted first-degree murder of Gloria McBride. The charge arose from an incident of domestic violence in August 2006. Dennis filed two motions to dismiss the information pursuant to section 776.032(1), Florida Statutes (2006), asserting that he was immune from criminal prosecution because his actions were a justified use of force. *Dennis v. State, 51 So.3d 456* (2006). The Supreme Court held that where a criminal defendant files a motion to dismiss based on the SYG statute, which relates to justified use of force, the trial court should conduct a pretrial evidentiary hearing and decide the factual question of the applicability of the statutory immunity. *Id.*

This finding became ground-breaking because although a lot of other states had adopted SYG laws by 2010, Florida became the first state to require the State to prove the lack of statutory immunity at a separate hearing. This new application allows defendants three opportunities to be found immune: before the initial arrest, at the SYG hearing, and at trial. Although the State can drop charges at any time, this provides three separate times in which they must affirmatively justify the costs.

Expansion of SYG: George Zimmerman

Although the facts of this case are very well known, and there were no significant rulings from the Court that changed the landscape of SYG laws, it is essential to include it here because this case served as a national landmark for SYG laws and specifically brought Florida's law to the forefront. The issues that have occurred since this one has undoubtedly been shaped by this case, and sadly, many states enacted SYG laws because of the results.

The State of Florida charged George Zimmerman, age 29, with second-degree murder in conjunction with the shooting death of Trayvon Martin, age 17, on February 26, 2012. Zimmerman was patrolling the neighborhood as the on-duty crime watch, and Trayvon Martin was walking home. It was dark outside, and Zimmerman called local law enforcement, assuming Trayvon to be a trespasser. Against the advice of dispatch, Zimmerman approached Trayvon, and a physical altercation ensued in which Zimmerman killed Trayvon. (Light 2017)

Initially, the Sanford Police Department and the Seminole District Attorney's Office refused to prosecute Zimmerman, but public pressure eventually caused a special prosecutor to be appointed, and second-degree murder charges were filed 44 days after Martin's death. Zimmerman was arrested and pleaded not guilty, claiming self-defense based on Florida's "SYG law." He was acquitted of all charges. That acquittal sent a message to the nation that it was okay to murder Black children, as a white man, because Black people are inherently scary. Many states liked this idea. (Light 2017)

Limitation of SYG: Burden of Proof

One of the few times that the Supreme Court has placed a limitation on SYG laws was in 2015 in *Bretherick v. State,* 170 So. 3d 766, 770 (Fla. 2015). On December 29, 2011, the Bretherick family was on vacation in Central Florida, driving toward Downtown Disney on a heavily traveled, six-lane divided road in Osceola County. A road rage incident ensued between Ronald Bretherick and the driver of another car, Derek Dunning. Mr. Dunning got out of his truck and approached the Bretherick car, unarmed, but eventually returned to his own truck without uttering a word after Ronald Bretherick flashed a gun. Bretherick's adult son then got out of their car and approached Dunning's truck, telling him to move, or he would be shot. Dunning did not move because he was under the impression that if he did, he would be shot. Several witnesses saw Mr. Bretherick's son holding the gun at Mr. Dunning when he refused to move and called the police. *Id.* at 770.

Mr. Bretherick was charged with aggravated assault with a firearm. He filed a Motion to Dismiss based on statutory immunity under SYG. The Supreme Court held that the burden of proof is on the defendant who files a pretrial motion to dismiss a charge pursuant to SYG law relating to justified use of force to show by a preponderance of the evidence that immunity attaches under the statute. *Id.*

Expansion of SYG: 2017 Legislative Amendment

In 2017 the Florida Legislature clarified the standard for SYG hearings. The Legislature disagreed with the decision made in *Bretherick* because the law provides for pretrial immunity hearings for Defendants where the prosecution has the burden of showing that the Defendant was not acting in self-defense by a preponderance of the evidence. The practical effect of this amendment is to make it more difficult for prosecutors to prove cases where a self-defense claim is raised. Since prosecutors have the burden, Defendants are not required to provide any evidence. Therefore, prosecutors will not know the Defendant's case ahead of trial if they can even make it over the high standard at the pretrial immunity hearing. This is the "second bite at the apple" Defendants have before trial, with the first being the initial decision to arrest or not arrest. The amendment is contained in Fl. Stat. 776.032(4) provides

> In a criminal prosecution, once a prima facie claim of self-defense immunity from criminal prosecution has been raised by the defendant at a pretrial immunity hearing, the burden of proof by clear and convincing evidence is on the party seeking to overcome the immunity from criminal prosecution.

This statute was significant for Florida SYG laws because it clarified that the burden of proof for SYG cases was on the prosecution once the Defendant filed a motion raising that defense. This changed the landscape for SYG laws because before this statute, defendants who raised SYG in many jurisdictions still had to present sworn statements about what their version of events was, and prosecutors would solely be responsible for combatting that defense. Additionally, because those Defendants were making statements under oath, if they did not prevail in the SYG hearing, the words they made could then be used against them at trial, which could have contributed to the reasons the Legislature decided to make a change. The implementation of this law not only makes it harder for prosecutors to prove SYG cases, but it also allows defendants to assert the defense with the judge and potentially be found not guilty by a judge without ever taking the stand.

BWS

While this chapter has been spent addressing the development of SYG laws through recent cases, it is also essential to acknowledge the development of BWS as a separate defense that has not been as successful as the expansion of SYG laws. This is in part because the SYG laws have developed because of historically patriarchal, heteronormative, white male rules, which were developed by patriarchal, heteronormative, white males. It is important to note that BWS is not a defense against crime. A person cannot be acquitted because they show they were suffering from BWS. Instead, BWS is evidence to show that some other reason should be applied.

It is also important to note that BWS, unlike the Castle Doctrine and SYG, has never been addressed or codified by the Florida legislature. It is not surprising that the Legislature refuses to acknowledge the plight of these women, nor to see the results of the cases that use BWS, but it is essential to look at them in context anyway to show how drastic the differences are between this defense and SYG, which is traditionally asserted successfully primarily by white men. The reason that BWS terminology is not updated to the language of IPV is that the law never edited it, not surprisingly.

Defining BWS

One of the earliest cases of BWS was asserted in Florida in 1985, long after the implementation of the Castle Doctrine, and because during this period, the *Bobbit/Conner* ruling was still in effect. By this time, Lenore Walker was an established expert on BWS and had many publications related to the issue. She was hired as an expert to testify in the case of *Hawthorne v. State*, 470 So. 2d 770 (Fla. Dist. Ct. App. 1985). Mrs. Hawthorne was tried three times for the murder of her husband. In the first trial, Mrs. Hawthorne's evidence of BWS was admitted, and she was convicted of the lesser included charge of manslaughter. In both Mrs. Hawthorne's second and third trials, the testimony from Lenore Walker was excluded. After the second trial, the Court found that the testimony should have been admitted because she raised self-defense, which required her to show that she believed it was necessary for her to use deadly force against her husband to prevent imminent death or great bodily harm to herself or her children. *Hawthorne*, 408 So.2d at 807. After the third trial, where Lenore Walker's testimony was again excluded, the Court held that refusal to admit the testimony of a witness who was an expert in the field of study known as the "BWS" was based on the conclusion that depth of study in the area had not yet reached a point where an expert could give testimony with any degree of assurance and was not an abuse of discretion. The case was overturned on other grounds, but the results are not clear. What is known is that Mrs. Hawthorne never served prison time for the offense.

This decision was very impactful in understanding where the courts were in accepting BWS. Even after the court ruled the evidence should be admitted after her second trial, it was still excluded from the third trial. Further, despite the diagnosis being established in peer-reviewed literature six years before this case, the Court still held that the study was not clearly established. After this case, courts were hesitant to admit evidence of BWS. On the other hand, the castle doctrine was well-based and, in effect, primarily for men. Still, this ruling seems consistent with the holding in *Bobbit*, illustrating the lack of credibility that the Court saw in domestic violence cases.

Expanding BWS: Acceptance

The first time the Florida Supreme Court addressed BWS was in 1993, almost 100 years after the Castle Doctrine was introduced, in *State v. Hickson*, 630 So. 2d 172, 176 (Fla. 1993). Michelle Hickson was a Black woman who was accused of killing her husband. Ms. Hickson lived with her husband for several months and eventually married on July 1, 1990. Four days later, she stabbed him to death, and the state charged her with second-degree murder. Ms. Hickson's case was the first in the State of Florida where BWS evidence was admitted.

This case brought us three significant holdings from the Supreme Court that changed the landscape of self-defense laws for women who have been the victim of IPV: (1) If an expert is qualified to give an opinion on the subject matter, expert testimony on battered-spouse syndrome is admissible to support the claim of self-defense. (2) When the defendant relies on battered-spouse syndrome evidence to support the claim of self-defense, testifying expert can describe the syndrome and characteristics of a person suffering from the syndrome and can express an opinion in response to hypothetical questions predicated on facts in evidence. *State v. Hickson*, 630 So. 2d 172 (Fla. 1993). Although Ms. Hickson received a new trial, she was again convicted of murder and sentenced to 22 years in prison. Ms. Hickson's case illustrates the difficulty with BWS in that even if a Court rules in your favor, a jury still has the ultimate decision, and BWS does not provide a complete defense to any charge.

Another case that shows the continued acceptance of BWS is that of Kimberly Soubielle. In 1988, Kimberly Soubielle was convicted and sentenced to 15 years in prison for murdering her husband. The state charged Ms. Soubielle with premeditated murder, citing, among other things, the fact that her husband was shot seven times with a.357 Magnum revolver, three times in the back. An hour after the shooting, before calling 911, Ms. Soubielle attempted to place the body in the trunk of her car, according to evidence discovered by police. Ms. Soubielle stated that her actions were in self-defense. Her attorney presented evidence that she was subjected to years of physical and sexual abuse at the hands of Pierre and suffered from BWS. Ms. Soubielle testified that she suspected her husband of abusing their daughter, Allison, who was two years old. She believed that her and her daughter's lives were at risk. (Mason 1991)

The interesting part of this case was that it came after December 1991 when the Governor at the time, Lawton Chiles, and his Cabinet took a very progressive step and allowed BWS to become a basis for petitioning for clemency, stating that "any woman incarcerated for killing her abuser may now use the syndrome to request a waiver...." (Keating 1993). Although Ms. Soubielle received no judicial reductions to her sentence, in March 1993, the Governor and five Cabinet members voted to reduce Ms. Soubielle's fifteen-year sentence for second-degree murder to time already served, making her the first woman to receive clemency under the new guidelines. This case was significant because it occurred at a time when the BWS was becoming accepted increasingly and was now even recognized by the executive branch of government. (Keating 1993)

Next, we must revisit Kathleen Weiand. As stated previously, Mrs. Weiand was charged with first-degree murder for the 1994 shooting death of her husband, Todd Weiand. The critical thing to note about this case is that although it is technically a BWS case, and the Supreme Court goes to great lengths to acknowledge and accept the problems faced by women who have been the victim of domestic violence, the only expansions that are made to the law relate to the Castle Doctrine. The Court concludes that it was adopting a "middle ground" approach and finding that although a person does not have a duty to retreat in a home when they are in fear of great bodily harm or injury, however, they do have a duty to revert to the extent possible. This would have been the perfect time to address BWS and expand it to allow some immunity in some instances, but the Court declined to do that, leaving it to continue to play catch-up to the Castle Doctrine defense.

Limiting BWS: BWS is not a Defense

Although there was an acknowledgment and expansion of BWS for a time, those developments were halted upon the development of SYG laws. After this, there were no more significant developments in BWS. In fact, the following major rulings started to place more limitations on the defense.

On the night of July 26, 2014, Kristen Wagner and her husband got into an argument that turned violent. Mrs. Wagner had been drinking, and her husband claimed that she was the aggressor. She shot him with a gun in the lower back, but he survived. *Wagner v. State,* 240 So. 3d 795 (Fla. Dist. Ct. App. 2017). At trial, Mrs. Wagner's theory of defense was that she brandished the gun in self-defense but that the shooting was an accident. Although the reason attempted to introduce evidence of BWS, the court excluded it. She was found guilty and sentenced to 35 years in prison. *Id.*

The Supreme Court, in this case, made two significant findings related to BWS. First, the Supreme Court held that BWS is not itself a legal defense, but evidence that the defendant suffers from BWS is admissible to support a claim of self-defense when the defendant is charged with a crime against her abuser. This part we knew from previous rulings. However, the Court further held that evidence of Battered-Spouse Syndrome is not admissible in a murder trial where the defendant asserts the defense of accident rather than self-defense. *Wagner v. State,* 240 So. 3d 795 (Fla. Dist. Ct. App. 2017).

BWS and SYG

Since SYG laws have been so successful for White men, we are starting to see more women attempt to use the defense. This was the case with Catherine Pileggi, who was charged with the murder of her longtime boyfriend. At trial, Ms. Pileggi admitted that she shot and stabbed her boyfriend but claimed that she was a battered woman and did so in self-defense. Both sides presented substantial evidence to support their respective positions. *Pileggi v. State,* 232 So. 3d 415, 416 (Fla. Dist. Ct. App. 2017). Despite the Court allowing the testimony, the jury did not believe Ms. Pileggi. She was convicted and sentenced to 25 years in prison. The case was upheld on appeal by the Supreme Court. This case serves as an example that even when evidence of BWS is presented in conjunction with SYG laws, women are still fighting an uphill battle.

One of the few cases where we have seen SYG and BWS be combined successfully resolved this year in Hillsborough County. In 2018, Sabrina Hendley was arrested in Hillsborough County, Florida, for shooting and killing her husband, Mark Hendley. Her attorney argued that she did not want to shoot Mr. Hendley, but he was verbally and physically abusive to her and others the day before the incident (Ryan 2021). Mrs. Hendley, a white female, was taken into custody and charged with second-degree murder.

Mrs. Hendley's father testified that Mr. Hendley "sucker punched" him earlier in the day and that he witnessed Mr. Hendley slap Mrs. Hendley (Ryan 2021). Another witness, Lorelei Polatz, stated that Mr. Hendley put her in a chokehold, and she also saw Mr. Hendley threaten Mrs. Hendley with a "military-looking knife." (Ryan 2022). During an interrogation, Mrs. Hendley told detectives, "I remember getting out of the backyard, and I remember running down the street. And I remember him getting me and him pulling me back into the house. And then I remember getting back out again and hiding behind a car." She also acknowledged her fear by saying during the interrogation that before she pulled the trigger, she thought, "He's going to beat the sh*t out of me if I don't shoot this gun right now." (Sullivan 2022).

When Ms. Hendley shot her husband, only she and her husband were in the room. The Assistant State Attorney who prosecuted the case argued that there was no evidence Mr. Hendley posed an imminent threat to his wife. He noted that she told detectives he was "just standing there" looking at her. In other words, the imminence requirement of SYG laws was not present. When Ms. Hendley's case proceeded to a SYG hearing in 2021, the Judge agreed with the prosecutor

(Sullivan 2022). However, the case was later dismissed by the State Attorney's Office. In doing so, the State Attorney stated that

> We undertook an exhaustive review to get this right—including consulting with multiple experts and uncovering new evidence that was not available to law enforcement or our agency when the case began...We go where the evidence and law take us, and had we known then what we now know about the serious domestic violence Ms. Hendley had suffered at her husband's hands, she never would have been charged in the first place as she had a legitimate claim of self-defense (Marino 2022).
>
> After the case was dismissed, Ms. Hendley stated that "I ultimately felt like we were all

about to die," Hendley said. "If I had the ability to leave the situation, I would've left. But I did not. He had me trapped. And he threatened multiple people. I wish this had never happened. A lot of people do not understand this, but I loved my husband very much, and I do miss him, and I don't understand why it went the way I did." (Marino 2022).

The reason this case is included in this list is that it illustrates the difficulties with SYG laws and the imminence requirement. Although many feel that the right decision was made in this case, why did it take so long? (Sullivan 2022) This case, and the period during which it has been pending, is hopefully representative of a shift in our societal understanding of SYG laws and how they should be applied to women who have been victims of SYG laws. In an ideal world, the conclusion reached by this case will become the new standard.

The Imminence Requirement

It is also important to note that Florida's self-defense laws, even before SYG, have had a requirement that to use deadly or non-deadly force against an individual, the person using the force must be in fear of IMMINENT harm or injury. That requirement is present in the current Florida Statute Chapter 776, where SYG laws can be found. However, what is not contained in this statute is a definition of the word "imminent." This is important because in many cases that involve women using violence against men, women assert self-defense from the violence that did not immediately precede their use of force. By not defining "imminent," the Legislature has left the determination of the term entirely up to the Courts.

Two courts have specifically addressed the definition of "imminent," one before and one after the implementation of SYG laws. The first case, *Gaffney v. State,* 742 So. 2d 358 (Fla. Dist. Ct. App. 1999), involved a man charged with aggravated battery after attacking his girlfriend who lived with him. The Court stated, although as dicta, that for a victim's actions to be "imminent," the steps must be "ready to occur." In making this finding, the Court cites the American Heritage Dictionary from 1979. Further, the Court stated that the case could not have been one of self-defense because the victim's actions had already occurred when the defendant attacked her. While this case was likely not a self-defense case for other reasons cited by the Court, by concluding that "imminent" requires danger to be ready to occur, the Court placed a limitation in future self-defense cases that may involve women who have been the victim of violence. An alternate resolution that could have been taken by the Court would have been to allow the jury to make findings based on the facts. By including this definition in the opinion, it provides ammunition to be used against women in future cases.

The other case that has specifically addressed the definition of "imminent" is *State v. Woodson,* 349 So. 3d 510 (Fla. Dist. Ct. App. 2022). In this case, two incarcerated individuals got into a physical altercation. Once again, although the facts of the case may not support self-defense for other reasons, the Court made some findings that may have highly damaging future implications for women who have been victims of violence. In defining "imminent," the Court cited to Merriam-Webster Dictionary, which defines "imminent" as "ready to take place: happening soon." The Court then held that an "imminent" act "requires no further measures to manifest...and very little time or preparation may stand between the present moment and an 'imminent' event." *Id* at 511-512. Like the Court in *Gaffney*, the Court could have allowed the jury to determine if these specific facts met the definition of imminence, thereby not creating damaging effects for future cases. Or, in the alternative, construed the meaning of imminence to include situations involving women who have been the victim of violence and act in self-defense at a future time when they feel safe while still determining the facts of the instant case did not support a self-defense instruction.

Florida's SYG law is ambiguous as it relates to the definition of "imminent," and that ambiguity has now placed women at risk by leaving it to be defined by an unjust court system that has a long history of failing to believe or protect women. If the Legislature were to define "imminent," then they can resolve this ambiguity without leaving it up to the courts, which presently have defined this term in a way that disadvantages women who have been the victim of violence. However, in its present state, this issue demonstrates yet another way in which laws that benefit women who have been the victim of violence (a BWS defense) are evolving separately and unequally from laws that help white men (SYG) through interpretation by the courts.

This chapter has illustrated that the evolution of the Castle Doctrine into both SYG laws and BWS as separate defenses for similar actions has created two completely different and unequal discourses for men and women. These laws are all rooted in racist, patriarchal ideologies that have led to the unjust treatment of women in the criminal justice system. The Castle Doctrine, and now SYG laws, have developed at a fast rate and provide broad protection to white, male, heteronormative defendants while continuously excluding women. While this chapter has looked at the disadvantages to women as an entire group, the next Chapter will illustrate how these laws precisely and continuously disadvantage Black women.

Chapter Three: Black Women and Self-Defense

Telling the story of Black women who have been victims of IPV is difficult. This is mainly because a lot of the information provided by news media is either non-existent or wildly inaccurate (Simmons 2020). This then makes it much harder to determine their experiences. Not to mention, countless stories about these women go entirely unreported and defenses go untold because these women are continuously undervalued and discredited based on the color of their skin. Over time, we have begun to celebrate stories like those of Cyntoia Brown and Marissa Alexander, who have seemly received "justice" after being convicted of crimes. However, this Chapter frames the narrative differently: these women have not received justice at all and are being punished for actions that would be justified if committed by White men. This Chapter aims to illustrate how the criminal justice system has been adjusting its tactics in a mask of "improvements" while maintaining the same results for these women.

This task has proven to be much more complex than expected because so many cases receive no media attention. We like to think, as a society, that people just do not notice Black women, hence the line of research surrounding the "invisibility" of the Black woman (Jordan-Zachery, J. 2013). However, it is entirely plausible that these cases are not publicized more because those in power understand and recognize the injustices Black women have faced but choose to do nothing about them because they are comfortable with the results. So instead, they bury stories and hope the details do not become public, as we see in stories like Sandra Bland and Breonna Taylor (Frank, D.D. 2016; Smith, T.S. 2021). Then in the limited circumstances where the details do come out, we provide solutions that seem to be "just," "progressive," or "fair" but still subject these women to the disadvantages that plague all individuals who carry the label of "convicted felon."

Can we say any of the cases publicized in present-day media have done anything to make Black women feel safer than they did before rape was a crime? Do these results support the idea that rape against Black women is a crime? Has the law come far enough to allow Black women to go to the police while being abused instead of picking up a gun? When women, specifically Black women, see these cases today, there is no reason for them to trust the legal system. Black women are charged with the legal responsibility of "following the law," even when they are homeless, abused, trafficked, raped, etc. On the other hand, under the law, Black women receive no reciprocity by being protected.

This Chapter will illustrate this point by exploring the evolution of our legal system and the treatment of Black women over time, exploring the significant inadequacies that exist. We will see that the problems start very blatant, with women being killed and receiving no justice. Then, as time passed and these women were afforded a trial, juries provided them with no relief (this concept has never changed). The legal terrain becomes more complicated from here, but the results are the same. Courts have used mental health, redefined self-defense, justified weak legal defenses, and most recently used the nuances of BWS to punish these women.

The nine cases chosen in this chapter to illustrate these concepts were Celia, Marie Scott, Recy Taylor, Ruby McCollum, Marissa Alexander, Cyntoia Brown, Asia Simpson, Pieper Lewis, and Chrystul Kizer. These cases were selected based on the dates they occurred, with the earliest occurring at the beginning of the 1900s and the most recent is currently still pending. The stories of these women will help to navigate the legal terrain to understand better the adjustments our criminal justice system is making without improvement. These women are all Black women who endured some sort of abuse at the hands of men, almost all of which are white. This could be because research shows African Americans tend to be less sympathetic to victims of rape than Whites (Nagel et al. 2005). Since most of these women (girls) were incredibly young, they had to rely on their community to stand up for them. A community that has ultimately failed them all.

In six of these cases, the male "victims" were killed, while the "victim" in Asia Simpson's story was shot in the leg and survived. Marissa Alexander's story involved a woman who threatened her husband with a gun but did not injure him. Recy Taylor's story involved a woman who did not fight back physically against her attackers but had the strength to tell her story to the police. This case is included here despite it not being a case of self-defense because it changed the landscape for patients of this type, even though she nor any of the women mentioned received the justice they deserved. In all the other cases, these women were arrested, taken to jail, and were either convicted or their case is still pending. More than one of these cases has received national attention very recently. Although this research intends to highlight less well-known stories, these types of stories usually welcome little to no media attention, which makes it more difficult to gather any information related to the case.

What we see from all these cases is that whether it was in the early 1900s or the present day, these women are seldom believed in the criminal justice system. Even when their cases are reviewed, it rarely corrects the injustices they have already received. This stems from the laws that have been used as a measure of "justice" to evaluate these women's actions. The dichotomy of these cases, in which most of them show the women as victims and then defendants, all illustrate that Black women are not entitled to the law's protection, though they cannot escape its punishment. In the more recent cases, we will see that our society has started to acknowledge the inadequacies within the system and attempted to rectify them. However, these adjustments come too late, usually after the women have endured a considerable amount of suffering. The corrections are never the same "justice" received by their white male counterparts in the system.

This chapter adds to the existing literature in three ways. First, it illustrates how the criminal justice system is adjusting the laws surrounding Black women who have been a victim of violence but not making any improvements. Second, this chapter tells the stories of Black women in a way that is not traditionally done. Instead of critiquing every sentence these women have said, this Chapter starts by believing Black women and telling their stories from their perspective, as they state it. By doing this, we afford them a right they are not entitled to by most of society or in the courtroom. Third, this chapter provides a critical look at SYG laws and why this defense reigns supreme over all other defenses. This includes those defenses that have been put forth by these women during their trials and those adopted for them by lawmakers instead of affording them the justice and protection created by the SYG laws we use to shield white men. Finally, this Chapter explores Black women in a way that has not been done before: by explaining the myriad of issues in the criminal justice system that these women must overcome. When we fix one problem in the design, ten more present themselves. Therefore, Black women will never be seen or heard within the existing system unless it all changes. The cases are different, but the results are the same, proving that we consistently learn nothing.

Literature Review

While there is not an overwhelming amount of literature surrounding Black women who have been the victim of violence, either at the hands of an intimate partner or rapist, there has been some significant work done related to the topic. Stereotypes about Black women and their sexuality have led society to devalue their sexual experience. They have created this idea that Black women are somehow "unrapable," whether it is because people do not believe their stories or they do not see the bodies of these women as capable of being raped (Adenji, L. 2015). These experiences have, in turn, caused Black women to trust the system less and, therefore, not report instances in which they are abused (Donovan, R. & Williams, N. 2002).

Commonplace stereotypes and myths portray Black women as excessively sexual compared to Whites (e.g., Hooks 1990; Cowan & Campbell 1994; Sapp et al. 1999). Black women have been stereotyped as being more sensuous, permissive, and promiscuous than White women and having less need or desire for foreplay (McNair & Neville 1996; West 1995). Many of these stereotypes arose during slavery, from white men, to justify raping these women (Hooks 1981). For much of history, raping a Black woman was not criminalized (Hooks 1981). White men could fulfill their sexual desires while also increasing their economic worth with additional enslaved people when Black women gave birth as a product of this rape (Sood 2018). Black women's rape was an act that benefitted the economics of slavery (Collins 1993). Injuries to the enslaved were only equated to the devaluation of the black body for labor (Hartman 1998).

The justification for excluding Black women from being humanized came from two places. The first reason, an economic one, was based on the idea that slave populations needed to be replenished, especially after the importation of enslaved people was forbidden in 1808. This moratorium caused the value of enslaved people to increase and their owners to desire to have more. Therefore, they would have sex with their slave women to do so. The second reason is the justification for these actions. The idea that Black women have some insatiable desire for sex and, therefore, their enslavers sleeping with them was doing them a favor. This meant that the enslavers did not feel bad for their actions. This became a common belief in society, so much so that when Black women claimed not to enjoy sexual contact from their masters, they were not believed nor justified in taking any form of recourse against them (Pokorak 2006). Since this belief that black women were sexually immoral was so commonly held, the possibility of a penalty for raping these women was utterly non-existent. (Pokorak 2006)

The rape of Black women continued by White men after the Civil War, when slavery had ended (legally). Black women's sexual organs were often described as aberrant and less distinct than white women's organs, and consequently inferior, even in medical discourses (Haley 2016). These biases were, of course, also present in the law. Self-defense laws for Black women who have been the victim of violence at the hands of their male counterparts can be traced to their inception during the early 1900s. Before this time, most stated that Black women were explicitly excluded from any laws that codified the crime of rape. *Commonwealth v. Mann*, 4 Va. 210 (1820); *George v. State*, 37 Miss. 316, 1 (1859). In Florida, a case could be dismissed if the prosecutor did not specifically allege that a victim was white. *State v. Charles*, 1 Fla. 298 (1847).

Present-day effects of these actions remain. The systematic rape of enslaved Black people is still essential to understand the prejudices and judgments instilled in our society and still affect Black women today (Sood 2018). This explains why Black women today are still not seen as "legitimate victims of sexual victimization." (Tillman et al. 2010). Our society still finds it impossible to view the Black female body as an embodiment of respectable womanhood and virtue (Hartman 1996).

Multiple studies have shown that Black women suffer the highest rates of domestic violence (Caetano et al. 2005; Rennison & Welchans 2000). However, there are many Black women who either hesitate or do not disclose instances of violence (McNair & Neville 1996; Washington 2001), do not report the crimes to the police (Feldman-Summers & Ashworth 1981; Holzman 1996; Wyatt 1992), or ever seek counseling (Neville & Pugh 1997). The oppressive images of Black women, created by historical and present racism and sexism, influence the lack of reporting and even disclosure (Collins 2000; West 2000). (Donovan & Williams 2002)

Research further suggests that when Black women report crimes, they face additional obstacles from law enforcement and prosecutors. For example, when crimes against Black women are reported, it is possible that they are ignored, and even when the crimes are investigated, the investigations are poor (Ritchie 2017; Holloway 2014). One of the contributors to these flawed investigations is the fact that when police do investigate crimes against Black women, they frequently do not find them credible (Jacobs 2017). Even when Black women do convince police to file charges against a perpetrator, many times, these charges are later dropped by prosecutors (Jacobs 2017). (Sood 2018)

One article discusses Black women and SYG laws, specifically. The author argues that the stereotypes of Black women as fearless, aggressive, and lacking discipline, created through the years, an injustice has led to the exclusion of Black women from self-defense protections (Benz 2020). She tells the story of Siwatu-Salama Ra, a Black woman convicted of a misdemeanor charge of brandishing a firearm after defending her family, even though she had a license to carry it (Benz 2020). Although the article does not deal specifically with violence victims, the result is the same. Despite Black women receiving punishments cloaked in a veil of what people perceive to be justice, the sentences are harsh when compared to their white male counterparts who assert a defense under SYG laws, especially given that these women are known victims.

This Chapter adds to the existing literature surrounding Black women who have been the victim of violence by presenting their stories separately. The history of Black women's stereotypes and treatment make their experiences unique from any other racial group. Although all women have been affected by the lack of protection provided by self-defense laws, Black women have had to overcome additional obstacles that other groups have not faced. Therefore, the conversation must be specific to them. As Martha Minnow stated, "In critiques of the 'male' point of view and celebrations of the 'female,' feminists run the risk of treating experiences as universal and ignoring differences of racial, class, religious, ethnic, national, and other situated experiences" (Minow 1993, pp.47). The failure to at least acknowledge the effect of these differences erases whole groups of women from feminist discourse. As Darcy Burrell has pointed out, an analysis about Black women who have been the victim of violence cannot be complete without addressing "the vastly different ways in which the law...impacts women of color" (Burrell 1993, pp. 96). While this dissertation cannot address every level of intersectional experience, it will address the disparate treatment of Black Women. (Burrell 1993)

The Cases

This Chapter examines cases specifically involving Black women who the criminal justice system has failed, to show many of the different arbitrary avenues that these women have to overcome before they can start to receive justice in America. We see from all these cases that whether it was in the late 1800s or present day, these women are seldom believed, and even when their cases are reviewed, it does not correct the injustices they have already received. This stems from the unjust laws that have been used as a measure of "justice" to evaluate the actions of these women. In the more recent cases, we will see that our society has started to acknowledge the inadequacies within the system and attempted to adjust them. However, these adjustments come too late, usually after the women have endured a considerable amount of suffering. The corrections are never the same "justice" received by their white male counterparts in the system. These cases all illustrate that Black women are required to follow these inadequate laws or be subject to their punishment, even though they are not entitled to the protection afforded.

The Beginnings of "Justice": Celia (1855)

In 1855 an enslaved person known only by the name Celia clubbed her master, Robert Newsome, to death after suffering from his sexual violence for over five years. She burned his body to destroy the evidence. A search was initiated, and Mr. Newsome's body was found in Celia's home. She eventually confessed to the crime.

On more than one occasion prior to this incident, Celia asked Mr. Newsome and his daughters to stop the abuse, at least during the period while she was pregnant with another man's baby; but her cries went unheard. This was probably because no one could fathom that she was not actually enjoying the sex with Mr. Newsome, and if they could fathom it, they simply did not care because her body was meaningless. After Celia's confession, the local press repeatedly continued the narrative that she had acted without motive, ignoring the repeated instances of rape and pleas for it to end (McLauren 1991). Although she was only 19 years old at the time, she was tried for his murder. Her defense included a primary argument for self-defense, but the Court instructed jurors to ignore those facts. Her jury consisted of all white men who did not hesitate to find Celia guilty of the murder. She was executed for the crime. (Linder 1995)

Celia's story is short and supposed to illustrate where we have come in the development of our laws when Black women could not be the victim of rape. We will see that the stories of these women get longer, and the publicity increases; however, the results stay the same. In new ways, women are still being punished for being the victim of sexual violence at the hands of an abuser.

Overcoming Society: Marie Scott (1914)

Even after Black women were afforded the "opportunity" to be victims of rape legally, the practical aspect of society still proved to be a barrier to justice. Black women still had to overcome the stigma of being Black women, which meant no one cared about them nor believed them when they were victims. Therefore, the laws made no difference and could have just as easily not been changed because the results were the same, and in some cases, they are worse. An excellent example of this treatment in society comes from Marie Scott, who was forced to overcome the news and then society, a task that proved too daunting.

Like many stories about Black women in similar situations, there is no information about Marie Scott before she was involved in the act of violence. We know that in 1914 she was 17 years old, so it can be assumed that she was born in 1897. We do not know where she was born or anything about her home life. Her story serves as the perfect illustration of the invisibility of Black women. We don't know anything about who she is or how she ended up in her situation. Stories instead focus on her actions and seem to portray her as the person who did something wrong in this circumstance. Details about whether Ms. Scott had been the victim of previous abuse or whether she had some type of developmental delay could have provided an explanation about why she was in fear for her safety. Still, considering the historical period during which this event occurred, it is safe to say that Ms. Scott's story was never told because it was not necessary. No one cared who she was or where she came from, hence why those details have never been available, even to this day. (McMahan 2020)

What we know about Ms. Scott is that on March 29, 1914, she was living in "the bottoms," the Black-owned section of Tulsa, Oklahoma. Around 12:30 am on that day, Lemuel Peace, a farm boy from a well-respected family south of Wagoner, Marie Scott, was observed by his father spending time in the bottoms with a friend. It is unclear as to why Lemuel Peace was hanging in this area, but it was not unheard of for white men to be in that part of town to partake in gambling, drinking, and illicit sex. On the other hand, some reports state that the bottoms were on Lemuel

Peace's way home. Whatever the reason Lemuel Peace was in the area, reports state that his father saw him and told him to go home, a command Mr. Peace did not listen to. (McMahan 2020)

Instead of going home, Lemuel Peace encountered Marie Scott. The news outlets have never reported a consistent version of the facts. One news report states that "as Lemuel Peace and his friend passed Marie's 'shanty,' they saw her changing in her room. The half-drunk men entered, locked themselves in her room, and began assaulting her. According to a nearby witness Jason Harold Coleman, Marie's brother heard her screaming for help from the livestock stable where he was working and came to his sister's aid" (Equal Justice Initiative 2022). Other articles state, "Scott stabbed Peace after he and another man attempted to rape her: (Equal Justice Initiative 2022). According to one historian, "Scott's brother killed Peace in her defense, and Scott was arrested after her brother fled town" (Equal Justice Initiative 2022).

On the other hand, local press sources merely stated that Marie Scott stabbed Pierce without provocation and in cold blood, without mentioning why the White men were there or what they did while there. (Equal Justice Initiative 2022). The stories of Marie Scott in the media all present the facts in contradictory ways, using vastly different language. This makes it much harder to know what happened that day. However, a deeper analysis of the facts shows us some glaring red flags in some of the presentations.

For example, the *Tulsa Star*, a newspaper explicitly created for African Americans (Oklahoma Historical Society 2022), detailed the story on its front page and refrained from calling Ms. Scott "a negro woman." The newspaper pointed out that she was new to the area and had only come to the Bottoms two weeks ago. Although the story does mention that Mr. Peace was attacked without provocation, it also points out that the story seems very unlikely given that Mr. Peace was in the area where white men frequent for sex, and he would have had no other reason to be there

(Unknown 1914b). The story does not seem to have garnered any coverage in the city's largest white newspaper, the *Tulsa World* (Lukerson 2020). Further, in another white newspaper for the city, the *Tulsa Democrat*, the story received short, terse treatment by asserting, "That lynching will result beneficially to this community" (Lukerson 2020).

Another article, published by the *Evening World*, a newspaper created by Joseph Pulitzer and not specifically for Black people, detailed the same story on its front page on March 31, 1914 (Unknown 1914a). This article refers to Ms. Scott as a "negro woman" who killed a "young white man" by driving a knife into his heart. The report makes no mention of any possible motive, nor does it discuss why Mr. Peace was in her area of town (Unknown 1914a). Overall, what we observe is that the white writers who professed the greatest admiration for what transpired next were the ones who criticized Scott's actions in the harshest and most unreasonable terms.

At about 1 a.m. on a day between March 29th and March 31st (reports vary), a gang of hooded men came to the Wagoner County Jail. A jailer named Pete Ryan was told an officer was outside with some prisoners. He opened the door to several dozen men with guns who pushed their way in, took the keys, and opened Ms. Scott's cell door. Ryan offered no resistance. Ms. Scott was taken out of her cell and carried to the intersection of Main and First Street. One account claim that as the men took Scott through the streets, a rope was already around her neck. Her body was left for the sheriff to find after the men hanged her from a telephone pole in the city's heart. The Sheriff, Connie Murphy, finally showed up several hours later (Synar 2020).

Some reports stated that there were two investigations into the crime. One by Sherriff Murphy and the other by the District Attorney, C.E. Castle, although it is possible that Castle was a participant in the murder of Ms. Scott. Castle stated that a full investigation would be conducted, however no one was ever charged with a crime. Castle deflected blame by saying that he thought the participants were Peace's neighbors from outside the city. A "witness" later reported that Ms. Scott's mother, who remained in Wagoner, killed her daughter's other attacker (Synar 2020).

Marie Scott's murder occurred at an exciting time in the development of Oklahoma's legal system. Many news reports of the incident either failed to mention the possibility that Ms. Scott was raped or alluded to the idea that it would not have been the justification for her actions either way. This thought process makes sense considering that rape laws during the 1800s provided that men could not rape Black women. This was illustrated in the law, which defined a rapist as a man who "unlawfully and carnally know [sic] any white woman against her will or consent" (Sommerville, 2004, p. 148). "Know" in that context meant to have sexual intercourse with them. These laws were in place by the time Ms. Scott was raped.

Oklahoma law was then updated to be more inclusive by stating that "Rape in the first degree may be committed upon a female of any age when accomplished by force and violence overcoming her resistance, or using threats of immediate and great bodily harm, accompanied by apparent power of execution." Further, "Carnal knowledge of a female over the age of 16 years and under the age of 18, of previous chaste and virtuous character, other than the wife of the defendant, whether accomplished with or without the consent of such female, is rape in the second degree." (*Davis v. State*, 1920 OK CR 152).

This law could have been helpful for Ms. Scott; however, what we can see in this case from the information we do have is the constant victim-blaming nature of the reports, suggesting that Ms. Scott was a prostitute and, therefore, not deserving of justice under the law, although there was no proof that Ms. Scott was anything other than a woman of "chaste and virtuous character." Additionally, we all know that these laws worked differently for White women than they did for Black women, and the change in wording for the statute does not change that fact. A reoccurring theme that we will see in examining these cases is that it is hard to pinpoint specific laws that target or discriminate against Black women simply by how they were worded. This was a customary practice during the 1800s, but as the 20th century came, most legal documents did not expressly exclude Black women on their faces. However, we can see from Ms. Scott that they did not have to do that in order to accomplish their purpose.

The issue Black women face is not so much with what the laws say, as we can see in the Oklahoma legislation. Still, instead, the problem is that Black women are not believed in these scenarios, and even worse, people will find ways to somehow blame them for being in the situation that they are in. Even when examining the newspaper article about Ms. Scott from the *Tulsa Star*, which is supposed to be the newspaper most dedicated to helping the progression of Black people, Miss Scott is referred to as a prostitute on multiple occasions. The critical consideration for this narrative is that by referring to Miss Scott as a prostitute, she is no longer entitled to the legal protections of rape under the law because she is not "a woman of chaste and virtuous character" as defined by the rape statute. So instead of telling Ms. Scott's story from beginning to end (now we see why telling these women's stories is essential), the focus is on what she did to a "youthful White male."

There is not a lot of legal analysis to be done for Ms. Scott's murder for two reasons. The first reason is that Ms. Scott was not afforded a trial by jury as she should have been. Even if Marie Scott was somehow guilty of murdering Lemuel Peace, she should have been able to have her day in court. Instead, she was robbed of that by an angry mob, upset at a Black woman who killed her rapist.

The other reason there is not a lot of legal analysis for Ms. Scott's case is that during this time, the laws were not a central focal point for America, especially in the criminal justice system.

We can repeatedly see situations where Judges and juries made decisions based on emotions rather than what the law dictated. This is probably why Ms. Scott's killers were never brought to justice. While Ms. Scott's story does not give us the most detailed legal analysis, what it does provide is an excellent starting point for the evolution of our laws surrounding women, especially Black women, who have been victims of rape and other forms of violence. In the following stories, the law becomes more complicated, but the outcome for these Black women remains the same.

Overcoming Juries: Recy Taylor (1944)

Societal stigmas remain an issue for Black women seeking justice, even today. However, the constant pressure placed on the injustices related to criminal justice has led to changes in the laws. The continuous theme we will see is that changes to the issues do not lead to improvements. What we saw in the 1940s was that there were laws which were equal on their face, but still did nothing to protect Black women from people, primarily white men, whose patriarchal opinions about these women and their bodies still had not changed. One of the reasons that this was especially important was because of jury services. Defendants of crimes have a right under the Constitution to be tried by a jury of their peers (U.S. Const. amend. VI). However, in the 1940s, juries almost always consisted entirely of White men. This detail proved to be an important one because juries decide what the facts of a case are and apply them to the law in order to reach a verdict. Therefore, even when Black women were allowed to be victims of crime, legally, juries still found otherwise. This was the outcome in the case of Recy Taylor.

Recy Taylor, whose birth name was Recy Corbit, was born on December 31, 1919. (The Rape of Recy Taylor 2017). She was raised in Abbeville, Alabama, where her family members were sharecroppers. When she was 17 years old, her mother passed away, leaving her to care for her six younger siblings (The Rape of Recy Taylor 2017). Early in life, Recy Corbitt wed Willie

Guy Taylor and changed her name to Recy Taylor. The couple had their daughter Joyce Lee in 1941. The family lived in the "colored section" of Abbeville, Alabama, in a sharecropper's cottage they were renting. Ms. Taylor started going to work during the day when Joyce Lee was old enough to stay with family friends.

Unfortunately, on September 3, 1944, Recy Taylor chose to go with her friend, Fannie Daniels, and Fannie's son, West Daniels, to an evening service at Rock Hill Holiness Church (McGuire 2011). The group realized a Green Chevrolet had repeatedly passed them while they were returning home from church (The Rape of Recy Taylor 2017). Eventually, the automobile with seven young White men inside pulled up next to them (McGuire 2011). One of the men commanded Mrs. Taylor and her friends to stop walking. All the men were carrying knives and firearms (McGuire 2011). When Mrs. Taylor and her companions continued without stopping, the same man confronted them with a shotgun and made Mrs. Taylor get into the car at gunpoint (The Rape of Recy Taylor 2017). The men kidnapped Mrs. Taylor and took her to a grove of pine trees by the side of the road, where they made her take off her clothes (The Rape of Recy Taylor 2017). The men threatened to kill her and abandon her in the woods despite her pleading to be taken back home to her husband and daughter. She was then viciously raped by six of the seven men after they had blindfolded her (McGuire 2011). Then, like a piece of trash, she was thrown out of their automobile and left by the side of the road (McGuire 2011). Mrs. Taylor's sister implied that this incident might have contributed to her infertility because she did not have any more children after that incident (The Rape of Recy Taylor 2017, 17:46).

Mrs. Taylor bravely called the police to report the brutal assault. The Daniels found the Henry County Sheriff, George Gamble. Mrs. Taylor recognized the car her attackers were in, even though she was unaware of their names. Once all the suspects were found, they eventually all admitted to the crime (McGuire 2011).

The men argued that since they paid her, their kidnapping and abuse was not rape because no force was involved (McGuire 2011). The men were sent home after the Sheriff heard their confessions. An all-white, all-male grand jury heard the case on October 3 and 4, 1944. The jury decided to dismiss the case after deliberating for five minutes. Mrs. Taylor's home was burned down by White vigilantes the next day. Her father and brothers moved in with her family. Her father, Mr. Corbitt, would spend the night watching over the family while sleeping under a chinaberry tree in the backyard. He would walk inside to sleep once the sun had risen. (Chan 2017)

African American activists like W. E. B. DuBois and Mary Church Terrell, as well as writers like Countee Cullen and Langston Hughes, took up Mrs. Taylor's cause at the time, putting the governor under a lot of pressure (Chan 2017). The governor dispatched detectives, who discovered that Sheriff Gamble had made up the men's arrests. Even one of the guys agreed that Mrs. Taylor had been pressured, supporting her story. He said, "She was sobbing and pleading with us to let her go home to her husband and child" (Chan 2017).

A Henry County grand jury declined to re-indict the accused on

February 14, 1945. (McGuire 2011). After some time, the civil rights activists dispersed, and Mrs. Taylor's tale stopped receiving news coverage. With assistance from Mrs. Rosa Parks, she relocated to Montgomery for a few months to avoid reprisals for telling her story. Mrs. Taylor eventually relocated with her family to Central Florida, where she worked picking oranges. (Chan 2017)

When they relocated to Florida, Mr. and Mrs. Taylor split up, and he passed away in the early 1960s. Joyce, their only child, was killed in a vehicle accident in 1967. Mrs. Taylor had two more partners after Mr. Taylor, but they both passed away. She spent several years living in Winter Haven, Florida before her family was forced to bring her back to Abbeville due to her deteriorating health. Taylor received a formal apology from the state of Alabama for how the State's court system treated her in 2011, nearly 60 years after the incident (Recy Taylor, Rosa Parks, and the struggle for racial justice 2022). Recy Taylor passed away in 2017 at the age of 97. She was never given what she deserved in terms of justice. (Chan 2017)

Looking at Mrs. Taylor's case from a legal perspective, it did not matter what the law was. The most relevant portion of her case was that she never was able to experience a "jury of her peers." The Constitution guarantees this right to defendants in criminal cases (U.S. Const. amend. VI). While this worked in favor of the six men who were never ultimately charged with her rape, it worked against Mrs. Taylor. The laws surrounding Mrs. Taylor's situation were irrelevant because when the all-white male jury heard the facts of Mrs. Taylor's case, they simply did not believe that a Black woman was entitled to the rights of her own body over the white men who raped her.

During that time, the law in Alabama provided that to prove the crime of rape, the State had to show (a) an unlawful carnal knowledge of a woman by the appellant and (b) that such carnal knowledge was committed forcibly and without her consent. Title 14, s 396, Code of Alabama 1940. *Smith v. State*, 345 So. 2d 325, 327 (Ala. Crim. App. 1976). "Carnal knowledge," as used in the statute, meant "sexual intercourse, that is, the actual penetration of the male sexual organ into the sexual organ of the female." (*Reynolds v. State,* 146 So. 2d 85 (1962)). The fact was clear that the men that raped Mrs. Taylor had committed the offense, but they were given many ways around the law.

The Alabama Supreme Court, in a case decided only months after Mrs. Taylor had received news of a no-indictment finding for the second time, explained exactly why the men who raped her were never going to be held accountable for their actions. The Court stated, "to the effect that the consent given by prosecutrix may be implied as well as expressed, and the defendant would be justified in assuming the existence of such consent if the conduct of the prosecutrix toward him at the time of the occurrence was of such a nature as to create in his mind the honest and reasonable belief that she had consented by yielding her will freely to the commission of the act." *Taylor v. State*, 249 Ala. 130, 133, 30 So. 2d 256, 258 (1947). It is essential to mention that the Court simply did not want to convict these men because it was also a crime in Alabama for persons of different races to "live in adultery or fornication with each other," but the Court ignored that point. (Novkov, 2002)

This statement is interesting considering the very nature of what we saw in Mrs. Taylor's circumstance is a jury who felt that Mrs. Taylor's rapists were wholly justified in thinking they were entitled to Mrs. Taylor's body. This justification was based solely on the fact that Mrs. Taylor was a Black woman. This type of thinking represents a commonplace in society. The agency of Black women (Ms. Taylor) is viewed as criminal and therefore any infringements thereon cannot be the blame of whites. This is a common tactic instituted during slave times to reinforce the idea that these women, who were powerless at the hands of these White male abusers, somehow wanted to be abused since they did not stop it, even though it was clear that they could not. (Hartman 1998). For this reason, no law could have provided Mrs. Taylor with the justice she deserved.

What we can take away from Mrs. Taylor's case is the importance of victims' rights. These rights are just starting to be discussed after so many years of abuse that these individuals have endured. When we think about the facts of Mrs. Taylor's case, she was a married woman who was raped by seven men, all of whom admitted to forcibly raping her but said it was justified because she was paid, and her conduct supported their actions. No matter what the law says until we start protecting these women, nothing is going to change.

Overcoming Stigmas: Ruby McCollum (1952)

Further examining the history of self-defense as it relates to Black women who have been the victim of violence is that sometimes parts of the laws do work, and when some of the actors in the system see things going wrong, they try to correct those things. However, without all the pieces coming together, these laws still act as a prison for Black women because of the stigmas that surround them. For example, even when our rules can see that rape creates trauma, we need to intervene and confine these women in diverse ways instead of acknowledging that they have the right to defend themselves like every other American. Further, these interventions are so subtle in many cases that we do not see the nuances of navigating the system until it is too late. Such was the case with Ruby McCollum.

The Ruby McCollum story is not widely known, but remarkably interesting. In 2014, John Cork decided to tell this story in a movie entitled *You Belong to Me: Sex, Race, and Murder in the South*. The film tells the story of Mrs. McCollum, who was well known in Live Oak, Florida, as the wealthiest African American woman in town (Cork, 2014, 3:30). The story focuses on the events that happened after she met and eventually killed Dr. Clifford Leroy Adams. While the murder occurs in Live Oak, Florida, in 1952, the story begins much before that time.

Mrs. McCollum lived in Live Oak with her husband and two children. Her husband became extraordinarily successful through his gambling ventures and was known as the "Bolita King" (Cork, 2014, 16:25). Through this success, the McCollums came to know Dr. Clifford Leroy Adams.

Dr. Adams was known as the "People's Doctor" because he cared for people of all races and did not demand money from individuals who could not pay. He was well-liked by the people in his town because he made them feel comfortable going to the Doctor (Cork, 2014, 18:30). This is likely why Ms. McCollum initially became one of his patients. However, their relationship took a sharp turn very quickly (Cork 2014, 20:04).

Dr. Adams began raping Mrs. McCollum in 1948 after she became a patient. He continued to do so until he died in 1952. Mrs. McCollum never reported Dr. Adams because, during this time, Black women were not seen as people, and non-consensual acts between White men and Black women were common. It was an unwritten rule that if a White man wanted to rape a Black woman, he had the right to do so (Cork 2014; 22:45).

The rape of Mrs. McCollum by Dr. Adams was not the only accusation of wrongdoing he faced. In 1946, Dr. Adams was indicted in Federal Court for submitting false claims to insurance companies (Cork 2014, 25:19). He was collecting money for services that he claimed to have rendered to veterans. Still, he was not rendering the services (Cork 2014, 25:22). However, the defense presented over 40 witnesses, and the jury found Dr. Adams "Not Guilty" at trial (Cork, 2014, 25:37).

In 1951, Congress passed a law that required gamblers to purchase a gambling license (Cork 2014, 26:28). When Mr. McCollum purchased a license, his finances became a public record, placing their gambling operation in significant danger of being shut down (Cork 2014, 26:40). Mrs. McCollum started to come under immense stress because of this process. In January of 1952, she was checked into the Brewster Jackson hospital for 12 days after she was diagnosed with a nervous disorder (Cork, 2014, 27:14).

While all of this was going on, Dr. Adams decided to run for state senate (Cork, 2014, 25:50). It was during this time, while the McCollums were facing significant hardships, that Dr. Adams won his state senate race (Cork 2014, 29:17). This victory led him to believe that he could become the Governor of Florida, so he began campaigning for that seat, as Mrs. McCollum was going back and forth to the hospital for her severe mental health issues (Cork 2014, 29:42).

On August 3, 1952, Mrs. McCollum entered her blue Chrysler and drove to Dr. Adams' office with her two children. She went into the Doctor's office with a gun and fired multiple shots, killing Dr. Adams (Cork 2014, 3:30). She then got back into the blue Chrysler, where her two children had remained the entire time, and drove back home (Cork 2014, 32:50). When the police arrived, they found Dr. Adams, clutching a $100 bill. Police immediately traced Mrs. McCollum to the crime and went to her house. When the police arrived, she was waiting on them and tried to pay them off, as she had done many times before for illegal gambling (Cork, 2014, 34:09). Mrs. McCollum admitted to shooting Dr. Adams and told police where the gun was but stated that she did not know why she did it (Cork 2014, 34:39). When Mr. McCollum learned what happened, he died of a heart attack (Cork 2014, 38:30).

Mrs. McCollum was tried before an all-white jury (Cork 2014, 45:46). While this was common during that time, it is an important fact to include because defendants should be tried before a jury of their peers to have individuals that understand the defendant's perspective. While we examined the issues related to this Constitutional right when we looked at Mrs. Taylor's case, Mrs. McCollum was not even granted the rights she was afforded under the Constitution. This is an essential right for Defendants on trial because they are supposed to be able to relate to the Defendant to determine whether their actions were reasonable. This jury was not able to do that, as would become evident later in the trial.

Mrs. McCollum attempted to present her side of the events. However, much of Mrs. McCollum's testimony was suppressed, especially the parts about the relationship between Mrs. McCollum and Dr. Adams (Cork 2014, 49:15). Mrs. McCollum even alleged that her youngest child, Loretta, was the child of Dr. Adams. Still, the judge instructed the jury not to look when the defense attempted to point the baby out (Cork 2014, 51:31). The verdict was read without any display of emotion: Guilty of First-Degree Murder, which carried an automatic death sentence (Cork 2014, 57:19). It was clear that many of the jurors had their minds made up before the trial even started (Cork, 2014, 58:02).

The Florida Supreme Court granted Mrs. McCollum a new trial after they found the trial court judge committed an error by allowing the jury to inspect the crime scene, Dr. Adams' office, outside of the presence of Mrs. McCollum and outside of his own company for part of the trial (Cork 2014, 1:04:18; McCollum v. State, 74 So.2d 74 (Fla. 1954)).

At Mrs. Mccullom's second trial, the defense raised an issue of Mrs. McCollum's sanity for multiple reasons, requiring the Court to do a further investigation (Cork 2014, 1:05:18). The Court found that the defendant was not competent enough to assist in her defense and remanded her to the Florida State Hospital until she was clever enough to stand trial (Cork 2014, 1:06:22). She remained there until 1972 when the Supreme Court declared her "Not Guilty" because of insanity (Cork 2014, 1:11:03). She remained free for the next 18 years until she passed away in 1992, 40 years after the death of both Dr. Adams and Mr. McCollum (Cork 2014, 1:14: 18)

From a legal perspective, we see two major principles emerging from Mrs. McCollum's story. The first is the very bare-bones argument for self-defense and SYG laws. While this is occurring, we also see the case evolving into a fight for mental health and a simplified version of

BWS. The first argument, self-defense, would have provided Mrs. McCollum with a lot more protection if the law had evolved to protect women in these situations.

Self-defense is an excuse for a crime, whereas the BWS defense we will see emerging in the 1970s is a justification for committing a crime. The significant difference is that excusable crimes result in not being prosecuted, or at a minimum, should result in not being found guilty of the crime for which the person is accused. In contrast, BWS implies that the individual is guilty but because there is something wrong with the individual, they need to be "rehabilitated" opposed to punished. This rehabilitation is why Mrs. McCollum spent a substantial portion of her life behind bars (although their justification was slightly different since the Court ultimately said she was not guilty; she just paid the cost of prison beforehand).

The reason we must continue to fight against the difference between the two types of defenses is illustrated very clearly in this case. Mrs. McCollum spent years behind bars when she should have been free. Ultimately, the Court released Mrs. McCollum, but she had already paid a price too high for being raped and defending herself. Self-defense laws should be put in place for women in Mrs. McCollum's situation, but even now, they provide no protection for these women. The ultimate lesson we should learn from Mrs. McCollum's case is that there is a difference between these two defenses, a problem that is central to this dissertation. Instead of pushing for increased usage of BWS and IPV as a justification for a crime so that women can be like Mrs. McCollum, we should be advocating for an expansion of self-defense laws so they can be free from the confines of the justice system.

The positive thing that we did see from Mrs. McCollum's case, if there is one is that ultimately, the Courts did recognize that being raped over and over by a man, against your will, and being threatened mentally, financially, and emotionally, by that man, when you have a husband and children at home, is traumatizing. Of course, we know now that there were a lot of other things in this situation that created trauma for Mrs. McCollum, but in this extreme situation, we see that the Courts are starting to recognize that there is something that happens mentally to a woman who has endured the type of violence and abuse that Mrs. McCollum has taken, even though she spent more than 20 years incarcerated.

Once again, the biggest takeaway, in this case, is Mrs. McCollum was not guilty of a crime. Instead of finding her not guilty of that crime because she was defending herself, we (as a society) find that there is something wrong with her mentally, and to "fix" her we need to put her into a mental prison where she remained for 20 years; all because she was raped.

Overcoming Placation: Cyntoia Brown (2004)

One of the positive things that we have seen over time from society is the increased coverage that cases receive when Black women have been charged with a crime after being the victim of violence. These cases have started to garner attention from celebrities and news outlets, which place additional societal pressure on lawmakers and other decision-makers. This is seemingly a good thing because, in many cases, they do become political platforms from which politicians must answer their voters. However, this is again an example of change, not improvement, because in many cases, these individuals' actions appease the voters but do not provide the justice these victims deserve. This was the case with Cyntoia Brown.

The story of Cyntoia Brown is widely known through all the criminal justice initiatives created through her story. Still, it is essential to highlight the critical details in order to understand better the legal and societal implications that have taken place because of it.

Ms. Brown was the youngest of three children, and her older brother and sister were so much older than her that they were already out of the house by the time she was born. Ms. Brown focuses her life on the period after she was adopted by her parents (Brown-Long 2019). Throughout her childhood, Ms. Bown struggled with her identity, partly because she identified as Black, even though her parents were white. Around the sixth grade, Ms. Brown began getting into legal trouble for stealing, breaking, and vandalism. This eventually got her kicked out of school (Brown-Long 2019). Ms. Brown then began living with different people because she did not want to return home (Brown-Long 2019).

It was during this period that Ms. Brown was introduced to a guy who became known to her as "Kutthroat," but he went by the nickname of "Kut" (his real name was Garion McGlothen). From there, her whole life changed. She was fascinated with him when she met him, and it seemed as though he could convince her to do anything. This is likely because although she was only 16, he was 24 (Mitchell 2020). He first introduced her to cocaine powder, then after luring her in with the ideation of a relationship, he introduced her to prostitution (Brown-Long 2019). He convinced her that this was a way that she could contribute to their relationship. This training led to the events that ultimately changed her entire life.

On August 6, 2004, Ms. Brown walked to Sonic to get food after arguing with Kut, who told her to go out and get some money. A middle-aged white man in an F-150 approached her in the same manner as she had been approached many times before. She knew it was time to "do her job." He agreed to pay her $150 in exchange for sex. Ms. Brown does not remember what happened that night but maintains that she acted in self-defense. (Brown-Long 2019)

Ms. Brown told police that she was walking next to a Sonic drive-in at around 11:00 on August 6, 2004. Johnny Allen, a man she had never met before, approached her in a white Ford F-150 and asked her if she was hungry. Ms. Brown got into Mr. Allen's truck, and the two went to the drive-in. While there, Ms. Brown remembers one of the workers said to Mr. Allen, "You back again," to which Mr. Allen replied, "yeah." Ms. Brown believed that to mean that he regularly picked up women there the same way. While Mr. Allen and Ms. Brown waited for their food; Mr. Allen told Ms. Brown that she did not need to be "stayin' on the streets" and told Ms. Brown multiple times that "he was a safe person." He then asked her to spend the night at his house, and Ms. Brown agreed. (*State v. Brown*, No. M200700427CCAR3CD, 2009 WL 1038275, at *1 (Tenn. Crim. App. Apr. 20, 2009))

Mr. Allen then drove Ms. Brown to his house. While there, Mr. Allen showed her several guns, including rifles, and told her that he "was in the Army and was a sharpshooter or something like that." They then got into bed together. Ms. Brown tried to fall asleep, but Mr. Allen would wake up every five to ten minutes to use the restroom or go to a different bedroom. At one point, Ms. Brown noticed Mr. Allen reaching beneath the bed and said she thought he was attempting to pull out a gun. Ms. Brown shot Mr. Allen with a revolver she "acquired on the street" after reaching in her handbag on a nightstand to the right of the bed. *Id.*

In 2006, when Ms. Brown was 18 years old, she was tried for Mr. Allen's murder (Garcia, 2018). Despite her age, Ms. Brown was charged with first-degree felony murder and aggravated robbery as an adult because prosecutors believed Ms. Brown's true motivation was a robbery. During this time, Ms. Brown gained more knowledge about her birth mother. She learned that her mother was an alcoholic, which resulted in Ms. Brown being diagnosed with a fetal alcohol spectrum disorder. This disorder has been known to cause "poor impulse control and a disconnect between thought and action." However, Ms. Brown's attorneys did not present evidence of her traumatic childhood at her trial because they were concerned that this same evidence could work against her. She was convicted and sentenced to two concurrent life sentences. (Carroll 2019)

Kutthroat died in a drug deal gone wrong after Ms. Brown was sentenced but never faced any criminal charges concerning Ms. Brown's incident (Farrell 2020).

Ms. Brown appealed her sentence based on ineffective assistance of counsel since the attorneys presented no information about Ms. Brown's childhood or any of the complications created through her history of sex work, abuse, and fetal alcohol syndrome. However, the Tennessee Supreme Court denied Ms. Brown's appeal. This included a rejection to reverse the case due to newly discovered evidence because Ms. Brown would have to "actually be innocent," and they were not convinced she was. The Court further determined that Ms. Brown's sentence was lawful because a "life sentence" is defined as 60 years. The court held that "A life sentence is defined by state law as a fixed term of 60 years. However, by accumulating additional sentencing credits, the sixty-year sentence could be cut by up to 15% or nine years." In other words, the court determined that Ms. Brown's sentence did not violate the US Supreme Court ruling prohibiting sentencing children to jail periods comparable to death in prison because Ms. Brown's sentence was technically 51 years after credit, not 60 (even though that ruling assumed she would get credit, which was not guaranteed). Therefore, it technically did not constitute a "life sentence." (Carroll 2019).

However, after much public attention from advocates such as Rihanna and Kim Kardashian, Ms. Brown was released from prison in 2019. Gov. Bill Haslam ultimately granted Ms. Brown clemency because he thought the 51-year sentence was "too harsh." However, she was still given an additional 10-year parole sentence, despite being freed from prison. Her parole conditions included a pre-approved release plan, a requirement that she maintain a full-time job or be in school and attend scheduled therapy sessions. She was also required to complete at least 50 hours of community service, including time spent helping at-risk children. (Carter 2019).

Although freeing Ms. Brown was the right thing to do, it was for the wrong reasons. The story of Cyntoia Brown is much like that of Ms. Ruby McCollum. The sentences that these women receive are viewed as a "favor" to these women instead of the punishment that it is. By ignoring that Ms. Brown's actions were justifiable use of force in defense of herself, a victim of sex trafficking, we are instead condemning her actions but said the punishment was too harsh. Further, although her sentence was reduced, it was not nullified. Her conviction still stands, and she must serve ten years on probation. If this case were treated as an actual self-defense case, she would have been justified under the law for her actions.

Overcoming being a Black Woman: Marissa Alexander (2010)

As time passes, much of society likes to believe that the criminal justice system is improving for Black and Brown people. Phrases like "look how far we've come," "we are better than that now," or "we fixed that" have become commonplace. However, as the previous examples have illustrated, our system is indeed changing, but when it comes to Black women who have been victims of violence, we are not improving. The bottom line is that no matter how much we re-write the laws, society views justice for Black women differently from how we view it for white men. Further, Black women have to consider this outcome constantly, and even when Courts rule in their favor, they must fear that when their lives are left in the hands of juries, that is a risk they probably should not take. This is what happened to Marrissa Alexander.

Although Marrissa Alexander's story did not garner as much attention as the story of Cyntoia Brown, it became a landmark case in the state of Florida. It caused the minimum mandatory laws to be revised. Unlike most of the other stories presented here, Ms. Alexander did not shoot or kill anyone. In many ways, her story was a classic case of self-defense, but before we go into the details, it is essential to provide some background.

Ms. Alexander was married to her first husband, with whom she had twins. When that relationship did not work out, the two separated but remained friends and co-parents. In 2009, Ms. Alexander met Rico Gray after being set up on a blind date. The relationship was good at first. However, Ms. Alexander began seeing signs of aggression and control. Soon after, the physical abuse began. It got so bad that Ms. Alexander got a restraining order against Mr. Gray. However, like many victims, Ms. Alexander dropped the charges against him. (Amber 2020)

This abuse was corroborated by Mr. Gray, who told law enforcement in a sworn statement, "I got five baby mammas, and I [hit] every last one of them except for one." He also admitted in his deposition there had been "about four or five" incidents of domestic violence with Ms. Alexander before the shooting incident, including when he "pushed her back, and she fell in the bathtub, and she hit her head." He said that she went to the hospital, and he went to jail for that. (Amber 2020)

Ms. Alexander continued her relationship with Mr. Gray, and in 2010 she became pregnant with his child. At this time, the two decided to get married and work on their relationship to bring their child into a healthy situation. However, the relationship was still incredibly stressful. This stress was manifested in Ms. Alexander's pregnancy. She went into preterm labor at five months, and then at eight months, their daughter was born weighing only 4 pounds. Gradually, the two ended their relationship, and Ms. Alexander moved out. (Amber 2020).

A week after their daughter was born, Ms. Alexander returned to the home she once shared with Mr. Gray to get some of her things. She was supposed to meet her sister there, but Mr. Gray showed up with his two sons first. Ms. Alexander and Mr. Gray argued over Ms. Alexander's text messages. He accused her of cheating on him and questioned whether he fathered the child they shared. When he became enraged, she locked herself in the bathroom, but he broke through the door. She tried to escape, but he grabbed her by the neck and shoved her through the bathroom door. She finally got free and ran to her truck, but she could not get it out of the garage. (*Alexander v. State*, 1D12–2469)

When she realized she could not escape, she grabbed her gun, for which she had a permit, and returned to the house, holding the gun at her side. When she saw Mr. Gray, he immediately charged her, saying, "Bitch, I'll kill you" in an aggressive tone. In a state of panic, she raised the gun and took a "warning shot." (Amber 2020)

Mr. Gray left the house, and Ms. Alexander attempted to gather her things. However, the police showed up shortly after and arrested her. Ms. Alexander was charged with three counts of aggravated assault, which at the time, each carried a mandatory 20-year sentence. At one point, Mr. Gray decided to drop the charges, and the prosecutor agreed, but another incident happened between Mr. Gray and Ms. Alexander, where she ended up at the hospital due to injuries sustained to her arms from blocking his punches. Even though she was injured, she was still charged again and put back in jail after her bond was revoked because he told the police that she had injured his eye. Then the first case ultimately proceeded to trial. (Amber 2020)

During her trial, Ms. Alexander's daughter, younger sister, mother, and ex-husband all testified they had seen Ms. Alexander's injuries, which they believed Mr. Gray had inflicted. Two of Mr. Gray's sisters-in-law also testified that Mr. Gray had a reputation for violence in the community. The final defense witness, Mia Wilson, Ph.D., testified that Ms. Alexander met the "battered person's syndrome criteria." Plus, the jury could hear Mr. Gray's earlier admission to abusing her and all the women he was with. However, the prosecution argued in closing: "Now at issue is self-defense in this case. Remember, at issue, really at issue, in this case, is whether Mr. Gray ran towards her, charged her, and said, 'Bitch I'm going to kill you.' You must decide if that happened... What this case is about, ladies and gentlemen, is whether this defendant under the law was justified in her discharging that gun." (*Alexander v. State*, 1D12–2469)

The jury found Ms. Alexander guilty as charged, and she was sentenced to 20 years in the Florida State Prison as a mandatory sentence (which means she could not get released early). During this time, Ms. Alexander's legal team worked hard to get her ruling overturned based on a mistake made by the judge when explaining the law to the jury. Ms. Alexander was granted a new trial. Ms. Alexander accepted a plea bargain instead of enduring another hardship. She received a sentence of three years in prison, which she had already served, and another two years of probation, which she has now completed (Hauser 2017). Ms. Alexander's case also became part of the debate over the state's "10-20-Life" mandatory minimum sentencing laws, which require mandatory punishments of 10 years for firing a gun, 20 years for shooting someone, and life for great bodily harm or death. This case was used as grounds to remove aggravated assault charges from the 10-20-life minimum mandatory sentence, with the order now carrying a three-year mandatory sentence. (Hauser 2017)

Ms. Alexander's case received national attention. Many have compared her case to George Zimmerman and Trayvon Martin. Many critics of SYG laws cannot help but look at not only the similarities between the issues but the significant differences, including the results. Ms. Alexander shot a "warning shot" at her husband, who abused her multiple times. She did not shoot him, and he was not injured. She was acting against an attack that she felt was imminent and testified that she feared for her life. She was convicted and sentenced to 20 years in prison. On the other hand, Zimmerman is famously known as the 28-year-old White man who murdered a 17-year-old unarmed Black child, whom he initiated contact with after never having seen him before and, as justification stated, "they always get away with it." Zimmerman was not found guilty and has been free since based on the same law that convicted Ms. Alexander. The most significant similarity: The prosecutor was the same. Further, Ms., Alexander had a history of being abused by Mr. Gray and did not injure him. Mr. Zimmerman murdered an unarmed child. So it seems, the key differences between these two cases are the race and sex of the shooters. (Kenber, 2013; Deberry 2016; Mueller 2013)

Ms. Alexander's skin color denied her the right to be presumed innocent and the right to be assumed in fear for her safety. It is reasonable to be racist and to target people based on your presumptions stemming from those beliefs (if you are a White man), but not reasonable to defend yourself against violence at the hands of your abuser, even if the violence is imminent (if you are a Black woman). Ms. Alexander was forced to come to terms with this fact, which was likely a significant factor in her decision to plead guilty to the charges. She knew she could not overcome being a Black woman in the criminal justice system.

In reviewing Ms. Alexander's case, we can see a few positive takeaways. First, after her case was overturned by the Supreme Court of Florida, the Florida House proposed a bill that was passed in 2015 to reduce the minimum mandatory sentence on aggravated assault charges from 20 years to three years (Staff Writer 2016). This was a step in the right direction for cases with no injury done to the "victim." Now individuals are not serving 20 years solely for firing a warning shot into the air. Marissa Alexander's case served as a catalyst for that result.

The other aspect of this case is the self-defense argument. The positive effect of Ms. Alexander's case being overturned was that the Supreme Court acknowledged that Ms. Alexander did not have to prove that the victim suffered an injury to raise a self-defense claim. This seems simple; however, during Ms. Alexander's trial, the Court instructed the jury that they could only consider Ms. Alexander's self-defense claim if Mr. Gray had been injured. Since it was uncontested that he did not suffer any injury, the Court instructed the jury to disregard the self-defense claim. Additionally, during the trial, the Court ordered the jury that Ms. Alexander had to prove her self-defense claim beyond a reasonable doubt. This is never true since the State's job is always to prove the case beyond a reasonable doubt. The defendant simply provides evidence, if they choose, to show why the State has not met that burden. (*Alexander v. State,* 1D12–2469)

The problem we will see repeated consistently in these cases is that even if they are overturned on appeal, the fear has already been instilled in these women that they could be convicted again. This causes many women to accept plea deals instead of risking a trial again. This was the case with Ms. Alexander. After her case was overturned on appeal, she took a plea deal to avoid having to endure a trial again and was sentenced to the prison time she had already served, plus a period of probation. This is not natural justice because since she was defending herself; self-defense laws provide that she should have been found not guilty. Therefore, by pleading to the charge, it now remains on her record, and she is convicted of a crime she did not commit. In the criminal justice system, results like this are pretty common because people do not want to risk going to trial, especially in situations like Ms. Alexander's, where they have been convicted once and sentenced to a substantial amount of prison. They just do not want to risk getting the same result. That thought process is understandable; however, it is up to the actors in the criminal justice system to correct this error by amending our self-defense laws to protect these people. This analysis fails to mention or account for the fact that Ms. Alexander has already served time in prison for an offense she was not guilty of, whether she was convicted after the appeal. Still, we see from this case that the law is starting to evolve, and people recognize that there are defenses to certain crimes. Unfortunately, the results are still coming too little too late.

Overcoming BWS: Asia Simpson (2015)

Since Florida enacted SYG laws in 2005, many defense teams have attempted to use the laws in conjunction with BWS. In short, to prevail on a SYG defense, the fact finder must believe that the defendant was in reasonable fear of imminent Great Bodily Harm or death at the time when the incident occurred. BWS comes in because defense teams argue that the defendant was under stress from previous battery incidents. Therefore, they were reasonably in fear. The problem with this defense is it admits that a person in similar circumstances would not reasonably be in fear if they were not suffering from a mental deficiency of some sort. By presenting this argument, defense teams are admitting that there was, in fact, something wrong with the person, whereas a standard SYG argument rests on the assumption that most people would feel the way the defendant does. While we saw in Marissa Alexander's case that the laws work differently for Black women than for white men, using BWS as a defense still proves to be an uphill battle, as was the case with Asia Simpson.

Ms. Simpson was born on November 24, 1994. She was born and raised in Atlanta, Georgia, with her mom, sister, and two brothers. She was the second of her mom's four children. Her father lived with their family until the age of five, when her mom took her and her siblings and left him after suffering from his abuse. Ms. Simpson moved to Florida in April of 2014, when she was 19 years old, to attend college in Orlando. She initially stayed in a homeless shelter in Orlando for young adults between 18 and 21. She got a job working at Discovery Cove and shortly after, in December of 2014, began working at Target. At this employment, she met Eric Livingston, a white male and the victim in the case. He was her trainer, an Army veteran, and five years her senior. Shortly after they began working together, Mr. Livingston asked her on a date, to which she agreed. She moved in with him about a week after they started dating. (*State of Florida v. Asia Simpson*, 2015-CF-015442)

The two started living in Mr. Livingston's apartment together initially. Still, a month after they began dating, Ms. Simpson got her apartment, and they moved into that one together also, although the lease was not joint. They stayed in that apartment for seven months, when Ms. Simpson was still working. However, after that period, they signed a joint lease together in a third apartment, and Ms. Simpson stopped working because Mr. Livingston told her not to work. After all, women should stay home and take a more domesticated role because of his religious beliefs. She testified that she believed she decided to stop working when she decided to stay in the relationship, but she did not mind staying home. When she started staying home, he became a truck driver. However, she stated he only kept the job for about a week because he did not trust her. (*State of Florida v. Asia Simpson*, 2015-CF-015442)

Ms. Simpson also testified that her relationship with Mr. Livingston began to change when they initially moved into those apartments because she could not move large boxes from the old apartment to the new one. During this incident, he became verbally abusive for the first time. She also testified about a specific event of physical abuse in late August or early September, where Livingston slammed her, placed his right hand on her neck, and shoved her face onto the floor. She testified to another incident wherein Livingston choked her as she slept, causing her to wake up. She further testified that after that incident, she slept in the closet because she did not want to fall asleep around Livingston. She did not call the police during any of these incidents because she thought each time would be the last time and rationalized his behavior by telling herself that he was just having a bad reaction because of his time in the Army. Additionally, he would always apologize by leaving notes around the house. (*State of Florida v. Asia Simpson*, 2015-CF-015442)

On November 24, 2015, Ms. Simpson returned to the apartment to get her belongings. She did not inform Livingston when she would come by but went at a time when she did not expect him to be there. She arrived at 6 pm and saw his car outside, and she realized that he was likely at the apartment, so she called him and told him that she was coming to get her belongings. She testified that she had a gun with her in her purse but did not make it clear as to why. She stated she took the weapon from the new guy she was dating. Once inside the apartment, she testified that he verbally abused her and made her feel intimidated. After she did not react, he moved around the counter with what Simpson described as a "look in his eyes" that she had seen before. She explained that she saw him look at her that way when he abused her on previous occasions. As he walked towards her, she pulled out the gun and shot him because she believed that Livingston would kill her and felt that this was her only option. It was not until after she finished work later that night that she reported the shooting to the police. Mr. Livingston, on the other hand, testified that she came to the apartment to convince him to let her move back in, and when he refused to let her, she shot him. (*State of Florida v. Asia Simpson*, 2015-CF-015442)

At trial, each side presented expert witnesses relating to battered spouse syndrome and whether they believed Ms. Simpson was suffering. One expert testified that she suffered from the syndrome, and the other testified that she did not. Ultimately, the jury found Simpson guilty of aggravated battery causing great bodily harm (count one). The jury also made notable findings that Simpson did "carry, display, use, threaten to use, or attempt to use a firearm," that she did "actually possess a firearm" during the commission of count one, that she did "actually discharge a firearm: during the commission of count one, and in doing so caused great bodily harm to Livingston. The court sentenced her to twenty-five years in prison. However, Ms. Simpson appealed the conviction. The Supreme Court of Florida found that the trial court abused its discretion in precluding Ms.

Simpson's attorney from asking potential jurors about their feelings related to battered spouse syndrome. They reasoned that battered spouse syndrome was at the heart of Simpson's defense. Because the trial court did not permit her attorney to inquire into possible juror bias on that issue, they were compelled to reverse Simpson's conviction and sentence and remand this matter for a new trial. (*Simpson v. State*, 5D18-1104)

When the case returned to the trial court, Ms. Simpson re-asserted self-defense at a "SYG" hearing. During a "SYG hearing," the Court judges whether the greater weight of the evidence shows that the Defendant was not justified in using deadly force. In Ms. Simpson's case, the Court found that the State proved she was not justified in using self-defense. This was a lower standard than the one required at a trial, but once she lost that hearing, the only way for her to prove her case would have been to endure a second trial. Therefore, she accepted a plea of 5 years in prison, with credit for the time she served previously (*State of Florida v. Asia Simpson,* 2015-CF-015442). As of March 2022, she is still incarcerated, with a release date to be set. (Florida Department of Corrections, 2022)

This case is important to highlight because it shows how BWS is currently being used in conjunction with SYG laws, but to no avail. To prove that someone is acting in self-defense under Fla. Stat. 776.012, the State must DISPROVE that the defendant "reasonably believed that using or threatening to use such force was necessary to prevent imminent death or great bodily harm to himself or herself..."

The current trend in cases of IPV is to present evidence of BWS to show that the Defendants did, in fact, reasonably believe that the force was necessary. In Florida, "the law does not ascribe a subjective standard as to a defendant's state of mind but concerns a reasonably prudent person's state of mind." *Reimel v. State*, 532 So.2d 16, 18 (Fla. 5th DCA 1988). Further, "[t]he question of self-defense is one of fact and is one for the jury to decide where the facts are disputed."

Dias v. State, 812 So.2d 487, 491 (Fla. 4th DCA 2002). [A] person in the exercise of his right of self-defense may use 'only such force as a reasonable person, situated as he was and knowing what he knew, would have used under like circumstances.'" (Quoting *People v. Moody*, 62 Cal.App.2d 18, 143 P.2d 978, 980 (1943))); see also *Chaffin v. State*, 121 So.3d 608 (Fla. 4th DCA 2013) For this reason, defense teams present evidence of BWS then argue that someone in a comparable situation would conduct themselves in the same way.

This is a problem, as we see in Ms. Simpson's case, that juries in many cases do not believe BWS gives individuals a right to harm their partner. This becomes even more difficult for Black women who are already perceived as angry and aggressive. It is as though BWS does a disservice to these women by acknowledging their guilt because it is not reasonable for them to defend themselves and then ask for leniency based on their mental condition. Leniency that Black women are not likely to be given. Therefore, instead of focusing on BWS. We need to focus on amending the SYG instruction, which says an individual must be in fear of IMMINENT great bodily harm. We can see this nuance with Ms. Simpson. She was forced to choose between using BWS, which does her a disservice or having to argue that she was somehow in fear for her life at that exact moment, which would have also been a disservice because we know that she had a weapon and Mr. Livingston did not. By amending the statute, these women can be rightfully found not guilty because they were, in fact, using the same self-defense that we see white males entitled to repeatedly.

Overcoming the Past: Chrystul Kizer (2018)

As we can see, the laws are constantly changing in ways that appear to provide more protection to Black women who have been victims of violence and other types of abuse. However, what we have seen thus far is that the laws are changing, but those changes do not equal improvement. These changes are continuing to the present day. Human trafficking has now been brought to the forefront. In 2021, a documentary was published, highlighting the fact that "one-third of the almost 300,000 girls and women reported missing in the U.S. in 2020 were Black", but most of the stories received little to no media attention (Nawaz & Reynolds 2021). Of course, the reason human trafficking was brought to light probably had more to do with the White children who were victims, but Black women can still benefit under revised laws (one change that has happened since Celia's case). Still, we have yet to see how these changes will affect women who have been victims of violence, especially at the hands of an intimate partner. One case that will be a good gauge of whether we can overcome our historical faults is that of Crystul Kizer, who currently awaits trial for murder in Wisconsin. Wisconsin does not have SYG laws, but they have a new law that provides immunity for victims of human trafficking.

Crystul Kizer's story is remarkably like Cyntoia Brown's story in many ways. Although Ms. Kizer had a happy childhood, she and her siblings suffered a lot of abuse from her stepfather. This could have contributed to the trauma responses she exhibited as a teenager. (Contrea 2019)

In the fall of 2016, Ms. Kizer met Randy Volar. Although she initially said she met him at a bus stop, she later admitted that she met him on Backpage.com, a site that has now been shut down due to the number of child sex trafficking incidents that started from the site. Mr. Volar was 34 at the time she met Ms. Kizer, who was 16. He started buying her gifts, complimenting her and taking her on dates from the moment she met him. Although she told him she was 19, they celebrated her 17th birthday together, so she believed he knew the truth. (Contrea 2019)

A few weeks after Ms. Kizer's 17th birthday, she was arrested for driving a stolen car and fleeing from the police. She spent 55 days in jail before Mr. Volar bailed her out. However, he made it clear that he was not doing it for free and was clear about the sexual favors he wanted from her in exchange. (Contrea 2019)

Eventually, Mr. Volar started to "sell" Ms. Kizer to other people on Backpage. These adult men would pay to spend 30 minutes with Ms. Kizer, and she would have to give the money to Mr. Volar. Mr. Volar was not new to these games, and the police had been investigating him after allegations that he had given drugs to and threatened to kill a 15-year-old girl. He was arrested for this but later released the same day without having to pay bail. At the time of his death, Mr. Volar was still being investigated for crimes, including the trafficking of children and possessing child pornography, but nothing had come of the allegations. Additionally, according to court documents, Mr. Volar is in over 20 videos sexually assaulting young Black girls. The police had also been called to his home previously about a runaway child. (Contrea 2019)

On June 4, 2018, Ms. Kizer pled guilty to the stolen car she was arrested for previously. Immediately after, she texted Mr. Volar and asked if she could come over. An Uber came to pick her up, and she went to his home, where they ate pizza, smoked, drank liquor, and did drugs. He initiated sexual contact, but she tried to resist because she no longer wanted to do those things with him. However, he reminded her that she owed him. He continued to try to have non-consensual sex with her, and the two struggled. Ms. Kizer was able to get away long enough to get to a gun that she carried in her purse and shoot him. (Contrea 2019)

Later that night, the police arrived at Mr. Volar's home to find him burned and lying on the ground with two gunshot wounds to his head. When searching for evidence, police were able to review Mr. Volar's credit card records to see he purchased an uber. After speaking with the Uber driver, they discovered the name "Crystal." This led the police to Ms. Kizer's Facebook page, where she had posted a lot of incriminating evidence about the crime. She was arrested and taken to jail, where she still sits today. (Contrea, 2019)

Under the Wisconsin Human Trafficking statute, §940.302, "A victim of Human Trafficking has an affirmative defense for any crime he or she committed as a direct result of the trafficking without regard to whether anyone was prosecuted or convicted for trafficking." Initially, the Judge in Ms. Kizer's case ruled that she could not use the affirmative defense argument in this case because it involved a murder homicide. However, this was recently overturned by the appellate court. The issue for the jury to decide is whether Ms. Kizer's actions against Mr. Volar were a direct result of the trafficking she experienced. (Shivaram 2019)

While Wisconsin's new statute seems to provide protection for "women who have been the victim of sexual violence," specifically human trafficking, it will be interesting to see what happens when the defense is put to the test in front of a jury. It seems Ms. Kizer has already faced substantial obstacles because she was charged with a crime despite the statute explicitly stating that "victims of human trafficking have an affirmative defense for any crime committed as a direct result of trafficking." We know that Ms. Kizer was a victim of human trafficking based on Mr. Volar's actions and history. Further, and even more ludicrous, the trial court judge ruled against her being able to use the defense at all, despite the plain language of the law. The Statute does not provide that murder is an exception to the rule. However, that judge decided to exclude Ms. Kizer from the defense of his own volition because he did not feel that she should be entitled to it. We already know from our history that Ms. Kizer is facing issues that a White man would never have to go through.

The overreaching problem Ms. Kizer will face is that it will be an uphill battle to overcome our legal history and all of the other issues Black women have faced: stigmas, society, juries, mental health issues, different defenses, placation, and all the other obstacles that have not been identified yet. This uphill battle is happening, despite the lobbying on her side.

Ultimately, we will have to wait and see the result. However, suppose the statute were written in favor of a white man. In that case, it is highly likely that he would not even be arrested, like George Zimmerman, and would not have had to go through what Ms. Kizer is currently facing, illustrating that instead of moving forward in our justice system, we are perpetually moving from one side to the other and coming back to where we started.

Overcoming the Law: Pieper Lewis (2020)

Cases involving Black women have continued to be highlighted more as time goes on. Their plights and the injustices they face are being brought into the spotlight because they constantly receive unfair and unjust sentences under the law. However, what we will see in the following story is that the same law can also be used to shield the actors in the system from their wrongdoing to relieve them of their culpability. As we will see in the next chapter, many actors in the criminal justice system fail to take accountability for their actions within the system and how they contribute to injustice because they pass the blame on everything and everyone else, especially this arbitrary factor that is masked as universal standards that we call "the law." This is the story of Pieper Lewis.

Pieper Lewis's story is shockingly like Cyntoia Brown's and Crystul Kizer's. Like Cyntoia Brown, Ms. Lewis was adopted at an incredibly early age. She had a happy childhood until the eighth grade when her parents divorced. Ms. Lewis stayed with her mother, who became physically and emotionally abusive. At this time, Pieper began running away from home and eventually became homeless. (Tumin 2022)

Through a series of misfortunate events, Ms. Lewis, who was 16 years old at the time, began sleeping in the hallway of an apartment building. This was when she met 28-year-old Christopher Brown, a small-time musician. Although he gave Ms. Lewis a place to live, he repeatedly made her have sex with other men for money and even signed her up for dating sites where he would arrange sexual encounters. This happened about 7 to 8 times over three months. (Tumin 2022)

During this time, in May 2020, Mr. Brown told Ms. Lewis that she had to leave his house while his daughter and mother visited. He said to her that she had to stay with Zachary Brooks, a 37-year-old black male. He was an acquaintance of Mr. Brown, and Mr. Brown said to her that he would want to have sex with her. While there, Mr. Brooks forced Ms. Lewis to use alcohol and other drugs before eventually raping her. She did not want sex with him, but she had nowhere else to go. Once Mr. Brown's company left, she could return to his home, but she had not seen the last of Mr. Brooks. (Tumin 2022)

On June 1, 2020, Mr. Brown forced Ms. Lewis to return to Mr. Brooks' house. Mr. Brooks was intoxicated when she arrived. She fell asleep hoping that he would leave her alone, but when she awoke, he was raping her, but immediately passed out again, likely because he had given her drugs. When she awoke again and realized what had happened, she saw Mr. Brooks lying in his bed, passed out. She grabbed a knife and stabbed him more than 30 times before leaving in his car and going back to Mr. Brown's home while hitting some parked cars. (Tumin 2022)

Mr. Brown helped her clean the car and sell Mr. Brooks's sneakers. A maintenance person found Mr. Brooks's body, and Ms. Lewis was arrested the next day. She never spoke to Mr. Brown again, and to date, he has not been charged with any crimes. (Tumin 2022)

"I took a person's life," she said. "My intentions that day were not just to go out and take somebody's life. In my mind, I felt that I wasn't safe, and I felt that I was in danger, which resulted in the acts. But it does not take away from the fact that a crime was committed." Ms. Lewis said in her sentencing statement. (Tumin 2022)

In exchange for a guilty plea, Pieper Lewis earned a deferred judgment and five years of probation. A deferred sentence allowed her to get her record cleared after finishing the terms and conditions. Along with performing 1,200 hours of community service, the judge mandated that she pay almost $4,000 in fines. She also had to reside at the Fresh Start Women's Center throughout her probation, submit to GPS (Global Positioning System) tracking, and pay $150,000 in damages for the death of Zachary Brooks, her victim. Since the case was resolved, Ms. Lewis' has had a GoFundMe page set up that has raised enough money to cover all court costs and send Ms. Lewis to college. Since the publishing of this case, however, Ms. Lewis has been rearrested for running away from the Women's Center and now faces a new sentencing hearing (Andone, 2022). (Tumin 2022)

While this case may superficially seem to have a successful conclusion since Ms. Lewis is not facing any prison time right now, we have to remember that she was 15 at the time that it happened and 17 at the time of sentencing, meaning that she has already spent over two years in a detention center. Additionally, Ms. Pieper was charged as an adult with voluntary manslaughter and willful injury, both charges for which she now has a criminal conviction. Even if the case is ultimately deleted, she is on probation for the next five years, so there still is no justice. Additionally, this case received national attention, so unless Ms. Pieper changes her name, she will never be able to escape this story, not to mention the physical and emotional trauma that she has continued to endure. So once again, while this story may seem to have a successful conclusion, we must not get caught up in that narrative because if this were a woman of another race or a person of another gender, she never would have been charged while one of her abusers walks free.

It is important to note that since this story gained national attention, Ms. Pieper has been re-arrested for escaping from a detention center and is now looking to be sentenced to the entire length of the suspended sentence (Andone 2022). This is why a deferred sentence differs from an acquittal and we should not celebrate them like they are.

The reason the law is critical in this instance deals with why Ms. Lewis's case made national headlines, the $150,000 in restitution to Mr. Brooks's family. The judge stated that "this court is presented with no other option," noting that restitution is mandatory under Iowa law that has been upheld by the Iowa Supreme Court. However, Ms. Lewis' attorney argued that Mr. Brooks' rape of Lewis made him more than 51% responsible for his own death (Tumin 2022). If the judge had agreed with this argument, it would have alleviated the need to pay restitution to Mr. Brook's family. However, the judge rejected this argument and ordered Lewis to pay $150,000 to Brooks' estate (Tumin 2022). Not to mention, there are a thousand other legal avenues that the judge could have explored before sentencing Ms. Lewis as an adult, for example, potential juvenile sanctions to prevent her from having felonies on her record or a sentence to the time she served in detention as a juvenile based on the facts of the case. While the judge may not be able to dismiss a case, their hands are not entirely "tied." (The prosecutor could have dismissed the case, but they did not make a comment as to their basis for proceeding with the matter. Therefore, I will use the judge for this example).

The reason this is important is that we see a judge who can rule the way he wants to lead and use "the law" as justification to take the blame from himself. While the law may require specific conditions, and judges must abide by those conditions, many things about the law are subject to interpretation. However, we constantly see "the law" used as an excuse in criminal justice to account for and continuously allow the disparate treatment of minorities in general, and in this instance, Black women who have been the victim of violence.

Analysis

All the cases discussed above show a similar pattern of Black women who are allowed to be treated like property. Starting in the early 1900s, we can see that Black women have been expected to tolerate abuse. In situations when they tried to stand up for themselves, they were jailed and even killed. Although some of these women eventually had their convictions overturned, none of them were immune from prosecution despite the strong self-defense arguments raised by their cases. Even further, almost all these cases went to trial, and the juries also found them guilty after hearing the evidence of their abuse. It seems that Black women are simply forgotten about by the law and society, and when they are not forgotten, they still are not seen as credible (Crenshaw 1991).

Crenshaw has pointed out a potential cause of these results. Because of the intersectional identity as both women and people of color within discourses that are shaped to respond to one or the other, the interests and experiences of women of color are frequently marginalized within both (Crenshaw 1991, p. 1241). These women are fighting a system of oppression that exists not only for women, not only for Black (and Brown) people but for Black women as a specific subject group. While we spend a lot of time advocating for each of these groups individually, little is done to address the intersectional nature of these cases. The laws do not protect women who have been the victim of violence, which is the argument of this entire dissertation, but we also know from the litany of other research (Finzen, M. E. 2005; Alexander 2010; Duvernay 2016; Wilkerson 2020; Solomon, Maxwell & Castro 2019) that the laws disproportionately affect Black people. It makes sense, and these cases show, that Black women still face disproportionate sentences in the criminal justice system.

Part of this phenomenon is addressed in "Private Matters in Public Spaces: IPV against Black Women in Jim Crow Houston" By David Ponton. Here, he discusses how African American women were erased during the mid-20th century, as it relates to domestic violence during the Jim Crow era. For example, when women would often commit homicide, it would be a direct result of suffering many years of physical abuse at the hands of their "victims." However, that was often left out of the narrative. These situations would be labeled as mutual combat, as opposed to self-defense.

Further, he discusses the media's attempts to reframe issues of domestic violence based on stereotypes and segregation to prevent them from becoming public issues (Ponton 2018). This argument can be seen in all of these cases. The stories told in most of these stories were based on actual statements made by the Black women; however, the prosecutors and Court in most of these cases misinterpreted the law and facts, leading to new trials for almost all these women.

Ultimately, this chapter not only illuminates the stories of these women, some of which have not received the attention that they deserve, but it also shows a pattern of their invisibility in the law. Even with the significant push against human trafficking, our society is seeing the expansion of situations covered under the SYG laws; Chrystul Kizer is still facing murder charges for killing a pedophile. We have learned nothing from Celia, Marie Scott, Recy Taylor, Ruby McCollum, Cyntoia Brown, Marrissa Alexander, or Asia Simpson. All these women are either dead or plagued with criminal convictions for the rest of their lives because they were abused and attempted to stand up for themselves.

Now we see that these cases are not publicized more because those in power understand and recognize the injustices Black women have faced but choose to do nothing about them because they like the way things are. So instead, they bury the stories and hope the details do not become public. Then in the limited circumstances where the facts do come out, we provide solutions that seem to be "just," "progressive," or "fair" but still subject these women to a different type of prison, the one that comes with a felony conviction, for the rest of their lives, like Cyntoia Brown's case.

What if other Black women who view these stories do not feel any more protected from them than they did 150 years ago when the law said it was okay to rape Black women because they were not people? What if Celia could see Ms. Kizer? Would she feel relieved? Can we say any of these cases have provided any relief? Would Recy Taylor go to the police when they are being abused instead of picking up that knife?

Those individuals that are against expanding SYG laws to protect women who have been abused are the same ones advocating expansion in situations that protect white men. They argue that expanding SYG laws for women who have been abused provides them with an excuse to kill men when they become unhappy. However, the counterargument is what is the current law doing to stop it. When women, specifically Black women, see these cases today, there is no reason for them to trust the legal system. Black women are charged with the legal responsibility of "following the law," even when they are homeless, abused, trafficked, raped, etc. On the other hand, we will see that Black women receive no reciprocity under the law by being protected, just look at Ms. Scott.

This Chapter adds to the existing literature in three ways. First, it illustrates how the criminal justice system is adjusting the laws surrounding Black women who have been victims of violence, with some instances containing both but not making any improvements. Second, this Chapter tells the stories of Black women in a way that is not traditionally done. Instead of critiquing every sentence these women have said, this Chapter starts by believing Black women and telling their stories from their perspective, as they state it. By doing this, we afford them a right they are not entitled to by most of society. Third, this Chapter provides a critical look at SYG laws and why this defense reigns supreme over all other defenses that have been put forth by these women and adopted for them by lawmakers instead of affording them the justice and protection created by the laws we use to shield white men.

Chapter Four: Interviews

The previous chapters of this dissertation have provided research to support the position that our laws, specifically those relating to self-defense, continuously and systematically disadvantage women, especially Black women, through many arbitrary avenues of justice administration. Still, the questions remain: why and how is this happening? Why does the law continue to disadvantage women even though we know the problem exists? What happens if we change directions and educate the individuals applying that law? This Chapter consists of interviews with actors within every branch of our justice system to explore the answers to these questions. The research shows threefold: 1. the bias against women who have been victims of violence, especially Black women, will not be remedied in the existing criminal justice system; 2. Changing the law will not alleviate the problem. While it may have some effect, existing cases demonstrate that arbitrariness and bias are still embedded in the system; 3. since the law does not administer itself, actors, including judges, attorneys, and juries, are forced to operate within a system that has implicit biases against women, even when individual actors educate themselves.

Ultimately, these problems have been created by a variety of factors. First, the separation of powers allows the various actors in the criminal justice system to remain complicit in the existing problems by pointing to the issues with the other branches of government. Second, the lack of agency to create change within the system limits those with even the best intentions and ideas. Third, the lack of accountability created by the previous two problems allows some actors within the system to ignore the issues they might have. Fourth, the politics of criminal justice, at all levels, but for purposes of this Chapter, at the state and local level, prevent necessary changes from occurring. Finally, the arbitrariness of decision-making and personal explicit or implicit bias combined with the failure to integrate social and gender theory into legal practice will make it impossible to correct these issues. At the same time, there are certainly more factors that have led to these conclusions; the ones discussed in this Chapter are derived from the interviews conducted with the various actors in the criminal justice system.

For this research, I conducted interviews with key actors in the criminal justice system to get an inside look at how these individuals perceive and address "justice and fairness." This allowed me to get a more comprehensive view of the entire system.

The interviews took place over Zoom and were recorded and transcribed. They were semi-structured, with some questions and some conversational aspects. Each interviewee engaged in a single discussion (between 20 and 75 minutes) consisting of open-ended questions designed to gather information about intimate partner violence, self-defense, and the overall operation of the criminal justice system. Interviews were assessed to improve understanding of how SYG affects cases involving Intimate Partner Violence. Participants included current and former Assistant State Attorneys for the Thirteenth Judicial Circuit; a Victim Advocate for the State Attorney's Office; a member of the State House, who was also a former criminal defense attorney; a political strategist; two judges, one of whom served as Chief Justice of the Florida Supreme Court; a former public defender; and the founder and manager of an intimate partner violence clinic, who is also a law professor at the University of Florida. The interviews were audio and video recorded. All participants provided consent for the interviews and agreed to the use of their names and titles; however, for privacy reasons, I have decided to identify them by title and pseudonyms only. All participants were people I had a professional working relationship with and knew my research focus before being asked to be interviewed.

The result of the interviews was clear. Due to heavy caseloads with a lack of time and separation of power, most actors in the criminal justice system find themselves limited in the results they can achieve towards equality and justice, thereby limiting their levels of perceived and actual accountability. This system continues to disadvantage women who are non-traditional defendants and require an additional level of care and understanding because our laws are based on white, hetero-normative principles that are not easily changed or overturned. The more nuanced a case or an issue, the more difficult it will be to receive justice because of the lack of understanding of some or all positions.

Trauma-Informed Workers

Victims are the only reason why any of these conversations are essential. I spoke to two trauma-informed workers, each with over 30 years of experience working with trauma victims, either domestic violence victims or sexual assault victims. From these interviews, I got an overview of the system and the difficulties for victims of physical abuse from a perspective that would be much more like that of the victim than any of the other actors. I want to start with trauma-informed workers because, from these individuals, I was able to explore the system's problems from a perspective closest to that of a victim. The trauma-informed workers helped to explain many of the issues with the system, which is most important. From there, the Chapter will try to assume that each area of the criminal justice system operates independently to show that these personal changes will have little to no effect without significant scale change.

As described by trauma workers, prosecutors were among the influential groups of actors in the system that cause injustices to victims. Prosecutors have the closest relationship with victims of any of the actors in the criminal justice system (unless the victim fights back and is charged with a crime). Therefore, prosecutors have a heavy responsibility to make the victim's process as smooth as possible. Unfortunately, it seems like they often do not uphold this duty. Instead, they fail to communicate with victims and offer lighter sentences to defendants simply because they are overworked. One of the trauma-informed workers I spoke to, Alex, is currently employed at the Office of the State Attorney for the 13th Judicial Circuit. She has been working in that position for over 30 years. When asked about what it is like for victims in court, she said, "I've accompanied a number of them (victims) in for testimony because the only reason they would go is if I went with them and I'd find myself explaining to them the criminal justice process; because the prosecutor wasn't, and it's like, how do you expect to support this survivor and keep her on board with your prosecution? If you don't meet her, where she is and keep her updated...and part of that is prosecutors don't get enough training. Their cases are too high. They don't have support...and honestly, PDs [Public Defenders] are more underpaid than prosecutors and way overworked... Can we just work out a deal and make this case go away?"

Defense attorneys were also included in the issues. For example, when the defense attorneys ask questions during depositions and trials that re-traumatize victims. Alex stated, "We don't have protections for that (traumatic questions) because the defense attorney has a right to ask whatever he wants." She also mentioned the defense attorneys' failure to resolve cases, making the victim wait in limbo for years. "I don't think that defense attorneys should take two years for a case to go through just because they've decided to have more cases than they physically can do. I don't think that's right."

The police create another issue cited by trauma-informed workers. Police officers are responsible for protecting victims in violent situations; however, they often take inexcusable amounts of time to respond to calls and do not take the process seriously. The second trauma-informed worker I interviewed, Beth, is a law professor at the University of Florida, where she also runs the Intimate Partner Violence Clinic. She is an attorney and has served her entire career helping women who have been victims of violence, from being a prosecutor to a clinic director. When asked about law enforcement's contribution to these women's trauma, she stated that the response times in many cases are terrible. For example, "…One call from survivors saying it's been 45 minutes. Is somebody coming now? Can you imagine waiting 45 minutes for law enforcement to show up… so that sort of huge decline in law enforcement response. And I've heard survivors say things like law enforcement comes for the second or third time and says, 'Hey, I told you to get an injunction, and you didn't. So why are you calling us?'" A 2015 study found that the national average response time to a domestic violence call was 8.5 minutes (Thorndyke 2015). However, an older study found that the time was 19 minutes (Holmes & Bibel 1999). The research on this is limited and not specific to Florida.

The trauma workers also cited judges and their failure to take these cases seriously because these victims do not get the justice they deserve. Beth recalled a specific incident with a judge trying to get an injunction for a victim: "the particular judge that was on the bench that day didn't like injunctions and didn't grant it. We have a judge on the bench now whose response to petitions is, 'show me the blood.'"

Beth and I also discussed the wealth gap. Usually, people in the criminal justice system have lower incomes. It is implausible to see wealthy individuals in criminal court. "You're only seeing a slice of life, and very seldom do you see people in the high-income brackets because with money, you can pay for privacy; and those few cases that I've taken or that I even as a prosecutor have been nightmare cases because the violence is bad enough that it seeps through the privacy." This notion of paying for privacy is not new and has been supported by existing research (Holahad 2019; Lichter and Crowley 2002). Ultimately, Abby and Beth both cited the complete breakdown of the system as the problem. As Beth stated, "I don't see how any of this is going to change until women have equal advantages to economic power, political power, to all the powers, because until women have the abilities to control their bodies, to have education opportunities, to have opportunities for employment, where they can make, where they can make comparable salaries to have childcare, so the hard decisions don't have to be made about who's going to stay home and take care of the kids, or who's going to have a more flexible job to take care of the kids. Until all that changes. I don't think any of this is going to change."

What we can take from these interviews is that the entire criminal justice process, from the police officers to prosecutors to defense attorneys and judges, is all the problem. Each niche plays a role in the traumatic effects felt by these women (Van Wormer & Bartollas, 2022). Therefore, a change in any area will not cause the entire process to change unless the change occurs in all these areas simultaneously.

The Executive Branch

The executive branch of government usually refers to the Governor (or President in the Federal system), but it also includes the actors charged with enforcing the system's rules. In this case, the executive branch deals explicitly with prosecutors and defense attorneys who are charged with enforcing the law. Police officers could also be included in this section; however, since I was not able to interview any of them, this section will consist of a brief excerpt of the literature surrounding domestic violence and policing at the end. Overall, these interviews have shown that there are a lot of aspects that actors in the criminal justice system do have control over, but also an equally substantial number of factors that each of the actors in the criminal justice system does not have control over. This causes individuals, especially those in the executive branch, to feel personally connected to "wins" but disconnected from losses. For example, a prosecutor, Chelsea, who has been with the State Attorney's Office for the 13th Judicial Circuit for nine years and is currently assigned to the Special Victims Unit, stated during their interview that the most rewarding part of their job was "the satisfaction of feeling like you've satisfied a victim; made their day, given them some kind of relief or a sense of justice in being able to see somebody who's victimized them, be punished for what they did, whatever that means in that particular case." We can see that there is a very personal connection to cases that have the correct result.

On the other hand, when cases do not see the correct result, we do not always see the same personal connection. This is partially due to the simple fact that there are so many things that go into any given result. As another prosecutor, Danielle, who has been with the State Attorney's Office for nine years as well and has served as the supervisor for the domestic violence unit, very succinctly stated, "I just don't think the system is set up well to support victims, but there are hopefully cases where we do." Statements like this show that actors in the criminal justice system are essentially preparing for the worst while hoping for the best. There are so many arbitrary factors that create the design and cause the results. These random factors cause the discrepancies that we see between case results of all types. However, these arbitrary factors that could cause a given result also lead individuals to lack accountability for results in these cases, as evidenced by that statement and others we will see throughout the paper. Since the actors are anticipating faults in the system, many tend to attribute losses to inevitability instead of looking at what they did wrong. This is one of the reasons why we do not see change.

This is not to suggest that actors in the criminal justice system do not take their jobs seriously or experience the weight of losing a case. However, the point is that it is difficult to know what to change in the future when there are so many things that could have gone wrong. When

Danielle was asked about the difficulty in making the community safer and finding justice, she stated, "The criminal justice system is where so many other societal issues come to a head. And so, we're tasked with fixing problems that exist, in my opinion. So far outside of... you're looking at poverty, you're looking at education, you're looking at specific housing policies that have kept people segregated. There are all kinds of things that play into it. And so, we can be as progressive and as fair and, you know, justice minded as we want to. But if, if the systems aren't in place to help people succeed, then you know, we're operating in a vacuum. So, then you're saying I'm, I'm within these tiny confines of what I can do that is right or wrong. And what is the answer? And it's not always obvious. Most of the time, I would say it's not."

What this section will show, from both the prosecution and defense perspectives, is that the jobs are complex, and everyone is making an attempt to do the best that they can. However, so many distinct factors make the job impossible. Furthermore, because of the impossibility of the job, these individuals have a challenging time figuring out and changing the aspects that are within their control because the system is not set up for them to succeed. Therefore, the problem now has become two-fold, with systemic and individual factors playing a part in the injustice.

Prosecutors

Through this process, I was able to interview four prosecutors. Prosecutors play a vital role in the criminal justice process, but they also have a challenging position. Prosecutors are the only actors that can choose to bring charges against an individual, and although a judge can dismiss a case for legal reasons, prosecutors are the only actors that can ignore (nolle pros qui) a chance at their own discretion. Prosecutors also have the choice to offer whatever sentence they think is fair, and while the judge can choose to accept a penalty or not, they are still required to support their decision with law. Prosecutors can use their discretion. To many who understand the criminal justice system intimately, prosecutors are the most influential people in the courtroom (Staff, ACLU 2022).

On the other hand, the fact that prosecutors do have so much power can make their job extremely difficult. They are charged with making the right decision, even when there may not be a correct answer. As one prosecutor, Ellen, who is currently an attorney for the City of Tampa but also served as a Bureau Chief prosecutor and Public Defender in Hillsborough County, stated during her interview, "The law, in general, is extraordinarily complex. Every case is extremely fact specific. I think that's part of the beauty of the law, but it's also part of the frustration because it's hard...to predict because everything is very fact specific. And then people can view facts through different lenses and view the same facts differently." This makes it extremely difficult to know what the right decision to make is in any given situation. Danielle added to this by stating, "we (prosecutors) are in the business of predicting human behavior, right, which is essentially impossible. Further, some cases just do not have a right solution, and then I think having cases where there doesn't feel like there are any good outcomes; I think especially with mental health issues, you may have somebody who is competent to proceed, but you can tell they are clearly struggling with significant mental health issues. And we just don't have the infrastructure (to support the solution)."

Along the same lines, despite the discretion prosecutors have, they are still responsible for operating within the confines of the law. This can create its own challenges, as we have seen with the self-defense laws. Danielle described the legal difficulty of being a prosecutor and added, "It's why prosecuting domestic violence is so, so difficult. You know, we're, we're hamstrung by the rules of evidence." Prosecutors ultimately have the burden of proving every case beyond a reasonable doubt at trial. Danielle and Ellen both pointed out that SYG laws should and do benefit women who have used self-defense against an abusive partner. However, Danielle qualified this statement by adding, "And that's where the SYG is not necessarily helpful because when you're the victim of domestic violence or intimate partner violence, you come at your level of fear in a different way than a "reasonable person." So, when you're looking at the standard and SYG, it's what would a reasonable person do in those set of facts, just to summarize it basically." This becomes a problem because, as Abby stated, "Unfortunately, we still judge, and we still blame women for everything."

Another factor that makes the job of prosecutors increasingly difficult is the same for all the actors within the system: there is an enormous workload without enough time and funding to do all the work that needs to be done. As a statewide prosecutor, Farrah, who was formally employed as a Special Victims prosecutor for the 13th Judicial Circuit for almost four years, said when asked about the difficulties in being a prosecutor, "it's the workload, it understands that they, most of the attorneys that are dealing with these cases, don't, unfortunately, have the time to sit down and do some sort of proffer with the victim or meet with experts or, you know, have the facts analyzed by whoever. And they're just trying to do the best they can with the limited resources that they have." In many cases, in order to really convince the fact finder, whether a judge or jury, that a very slight issue (such as Battered Woman Syndrome) should be treated the same way as other types of self-defense requires education, educating prosecutors, judges, defense attorneys, juries, everyone. Education involves a lot of time and money: two things the criminal justice system just does not have. (Brown 2004; Holloway 2014)

In order for prosecutors to really understand women who use self-defense, they would need to take time out of their already busy day to be trained, and although most Prosecutors' offices do provide training, the legal issues covered run the gambit. This training would need to be done during the already busy workday when prosecutors are already stressed about their caseloads. Farrah, when asked about her workload, stated, "I think I always felt overworked. Although the level of overworked, I felt, would obviously be much greater when we were in a trial situation since, you know, there's a lot of stress and a lot of pressure that's going to be associated with that type of litigation, I always kind of had a kind of latent stress and anxiety really all the time." Danielle added, "I think the nature of what we do is just overwhelming." This notion of prosecutors being overworked and having too many cases is not new and likely contributes to the injustices experienced in the criminal justice system (Gershowitz, A. M., & Killinger, L. R. 2011)

Adding more training to this environment may ultimately do more harm than good because prosecutors would spend most of the time thinking of the obligations that they are not meeting. This problem works against nuanced issues such as those involving women and minorities who have experienced violence and used self-defense because these issues require additional time and training that most prosecutors do not have. This is a very nuanced issue that takes time to understand. It is important to note that most of the prosecutors in the Special Victims Unit and Domestic Violence Unit are women. While increasing the number of minorities might allow a better understanding of some of these issues, training is still essential because prosecutors come from various places with varied experiences, so we cannot assume they will understand these issues. Without training, prosecutors (nor any other actors within the system) can fully understand these trauma responses.

Another issue faced by prosecutors is that defendants have the right to remain silent. This is a problem for prosecutors because, many times, they cannot get complete information about a case. Danielle elaborated on this and said, "We don't always know about the people that are charged. We don't know their backstory. We don't know anything about them. We don't have their mitigation unless and until it's brought to our attention by their attorney." This makes it extremely difficult for prosecutors to determine accurately and appropriately what to do in a case. Many times, decisions are made in cases based on criminal histories because that is the only information available to the prosecutor, even though a person's behavior cannot be accurately determined by their criminal history or lack thereof. Danielle went on to say, "You don't want to make assumptions about people and what's going on with people's personal lives, but also part of your analysis as a prosecutor is trying to assess what should happen in the case, in terms of a sentence or punishment." Additionally, many times, when women are the victim of violence and use self-defense, the prosecutor will not know it was self-defense unless she raises the issue. This is another factor that makes it extremely difficult for prosecutors to get "justice" in a vacuum.

Danielle stated that the most prominent problem prosecutors face is "victim cooperation." Many of these situations happen within the household, and without a witness, there is no evidence of the crime. In order to convict somebody, there has to be evidence. Therefore, when the victims choose not to cooperate with the prosecution, even if they have their reasons, the prosecutors are less likely to pursue the trial of the case (Dawson, M & Dinovitzer, R. 2001). As was stated during the interviews, sometimes convicting the abuser is not what the victim feels is best, so the system works for them when the abuser is not condemned (McDermott, M.J. & Garofalo 2004). However, when the cycle of abuse continues, prosecutors will be working from square one all over again.

For the reasons stated above, many times, prosecutors' offices have high turnover, which causes cases to get lost in transition. The higher the turnover, the less likely an attorney is to know about a topic that they have just received or conversations that were had prior to that new attorney arriving. It is also less likely that the new attorney knows what has already been done on the case, and there is a period of playing "catchup." One way to combat this is to ensure that adequate notes are taken while the prosecutors are in their position. That way, when a change happens, the newest prosecutor is adequately prepared for the role they are about to assume. "I think there's definitely a concern when there are vacancies, as far as who's going to cover cases. Our goal is always to encourage attorneys to keep good documentation and to make sure that their files are prepared for whoever might need to take over, especially if we know that someone's leaving. But inevitably, you know, when there's changing of hands, things are going to, not necessarily get missed, but you know, there's going to be gaps in coverage and things like that. Ultimately, the system could benefit from longevity in prosecutors. As much as some of us would like, there is not going to be a systemic overhaul of the criminal justice system, and therefore we need people to take the job seriously to stay, um, and work within the confines of a flawed system to try to do the best that we can, um, with the structure that we have."

These interviews showed the issues with turnover, and the policies and procedures put in place do not address the lack of training. As we can see, there were protocols put in place, including preparation and documentation, to help with the transition of attorneys. However, the lack of training and experience was not addressed. It seems that the attorneys rely on more experienced attorneys and informal training to do the job, as confirmed by Farrah, "Yeah, we did have a mandatory sort of meeting that just consisted of a couple of hours with the chief or the deputy chief of the division where we went over specific types of the case saw that sort of was the foundation for how we made determinations for child abuse, child neglect, things like that. But other than that kind of bare-bones guidance, as far as what we're looking for when we're analyzing those types of cases. Since we hadn't seen this before, there's no formal training. When we started, I did have an opportunity to go to a few conferences during my time there. But other than that, it was really just on the job and just dealing with things as they came." Chelsea had a similar experience, "So, when we first started in the division, um *redacted* did, various pieces of training for each of us as we all come in. We have a big binder that has all the information we need, but basically, we sat down, and I want to say, for two or three hours and did a question-and-answer session on the binder having to do with sex offenses and child abuse. And then other than that, it's kind of learn as you go." Ultimately, a more formalized training program could assist in creating a universal understanding of victims and trauma responses.

Defense Attorneys

On the opposite side of the courtroom from prosecutors are defense attorneys. Defense attorneys have unique roles in the courtroom and are the only ones in criminal court who answer to clients. . Judges determine when to dismiss charges based on the law, and prosecutors have complete discretion over what amounts to pursue (within the confines of the law), but defense attorneys are serving their client. Therefore, they do not have control over any significant part of their cases without the consent of their clients (there are minor exceptions, but for most trial strategies, this statement is correct). In addition to this more significant conceptual idea, defense attorneys also have a number of constraints within the system, just as all of the other actors.

One of the problems cited during the interviews was that defense attorneys, especially public defenders, are overworked, with many of them having caseloads that are double the size of what they would usually be comfortable with (Richardson, L.S. & Goff, P. 2013). One of the two defense attorneys who agreed to be interviewed, Grace, who served as a public defender for over seven years, when asked about her workload as a public defender, stated, "I certainly did not feel underworked. We were overworked, for sure, you know, just the sheer number of cases that you're handling...we had probably too many cases to handle." She also said all the attorneys were dedicated, working on average 50-60 hours a week. Therefore, they were able to prepare for their cases. However, on either side of the courtroom, overworked attorneys cannot provide the highest levels of representation (Page 2022). Furthermore, it is probably safe to assume that budgets were limited, which means that the defenses that could be provided were limited (Peng 2015).

Another constraint placed on defense attorneys when trying to represent their clients in court adequately is the rules of evidence. Grace explained, "There are particular rules about the type of evidence that can come out in the courtroom setting and specific rules on things that are not allowed to come out in the courtroom setting... It's not just the statutes. It is the rules. It is then the case law that comes out from the different district courts." For example, in the circumstances such as women who have been the victim of violence, evidence of prior abuse may not be admissible to a jury, depending on the case, despite the defense attorney's best efforts. She continued, "It can feel a little bit frustrating to know the information, but also know that you don't have a mechanism to bring it up in the courtroom setting because the laws in the rules simply don't allow it."

Along the same lines of legal constraints are sentencing guidelines. Sentencing guidelines are a set of standards put in place to establish rational and consistent sentencing practices within Florida Courts (Frase 2019). Like federal sentencing guidelines, the goal is to ensure that fair and accurate sentences are being applied to defendants in similar circumstances (Margulies L. et al., 2019). The sentencing guidelines look at the defendant's current charges along with their prior history and produce a number that represents the number of months that the defendant should serve in prison. Prosecutors and judges have the discretion to deviate from the sentencing guidelines, most of the time before a trial happens (they also have intention after practice, but it is a lot rarer). However, in many cases, it works to the disadvantage of Defendants with extenuating circumstances because they limit the justifications for reducing sentences, and even when corrections are reduced, the guidelines are always used as a "starting point" for the reduction (Painter-Davis, N. & Ulmer, J.T. 2020). Grace explained, "(Changes to) Sentencing guidelines could probably help because sometimes, everyone's hands are tied in certain situations where you want to help, you want to do something, you know that there's a background issue, but the prosecutor has these sentencing guidelines, and it's hard to overcome those."

Another factor that was not discussed is minimum mandatory sentences. Minimum mandatory sentences are sentences that are required by law if a defendant is convicted of certain crimes, usually those involving violence. However, it is essential to mention that in the same way, the prosecutor can deviate from the sentencing guidelines; they can also vary from minimum mandatory sentences. The only difference is that the judge cannot deviate from compulsory minimum sentences, but they can differ from sentencing guidelines if they make "special findings." (Matheny 2012; Frase 2019)

Another factor that makes the criminal justice system unequal and inefficient is, specifically, the discretion of judges. The second defense attorney I was able to interview, Hope, was a defense attorney for more than eight years and now serves as the first black female queer State Representative; she explained her experience with discretion "I watched how the court dealt with Black defendants and dealt with White defendants; completely two different things. And sometimes, if they were charged similarly, the sentence wouldn't be the same. We're aware there was a report in the *Sarasota Herald* (Braga 2022) a few years ago that, you know, they took these two young men with the same record, basically, same charge, one got probation, one guy prison, the person that got prison was Black. The person that got probation was White, and this wasn't a one-off; this was a thing that happened. And I've been lucky enough to practice around the state.

And you can really see, especially in the smaller, redder, more Republican districts, that there is a great disparity on how defendants of color are treated."

Similar to judicial discretion, selective policing is another problem faced by both prosecutors and defense attorneys (McCartney, S. & Parent, R. 2015). Prosecutors, except in rare instances, only get cases that are brought to them by law enforcement., Therefore law enforcement plays such a critical role in this process because if they determine that a woman is not guilty under the SYG or other self-defense provisions of the law, then prosecutors and defense attorneys will never see the case. It is imperative for police officers to become fully aware of what is happening in a situation before making an arrest, especially in domestic violence situations. Grace explained, "If there was maybe a little more time taken in the situations than making arrests, maybe the police can learn information to know that maybe an arrest doesn't need to be made here; something else needs to be happening. So, we're not clogging up the jail. We're not clogging up the court system with an unnecessary arrest."

Police Officers

Although I did not interview police officers directly, they are critical to the criminal justice process and, therefore, necessary to include in this analysis. Fortunately, there has already been significant research concerning police officers and their attitudes toward domestic violence that will be included in this section. Few people would be able to successfully argue that police officers do not have a difficult job, and many factors complicate their jobs even further. These factors show that even police officers with the best intentions can still fail to create change within the system.

One factor that makes it increasingly difficult for police officers to handle domestic violence cases appropriately and efficiently is the mandatory arrest mandate requiring arrests in domestic violence cases (Bridgett, A. 2022). These laws require an arrest to be made in patients with domestic violence accusations are made. This means that police officers are required to make a determination on the scene as to what happened during an incident, that one individual is at fault, then arrest that individual. The benefit of this mandate is it does mitigate some of the violence that may be caused by leaving both parties in the home during a very volatile situation, which will likely get worse. However, the overarching problem with this mandate is that it requires an arrest to be made at the scene when the officer may not have complete information about the situation (Bridgett, A. 2022). Most of the police officers who were interviewed for a 2011 study said they had trouble figuring out who the primary aggressor was during these calls. Supervisors were more likely to agree that it is hard to determine the primary aggressor. A study done in the 1970s interviewed police officers in Philadelphia determined why police officers were frustrated they were with domestics. The results indicated that it was challenging to resolve complicated family disputes that had been going on for weeks, months, or even years (Rubenstein 1973; Blaney 2010). Given this information, it is easier to see why policies requiring police officers to make arrests can make their jobs more difficult.

Another factor that significantly affects police officers and their ability to manage domestic violence cases effectively is that they are not the ultimate decision-maker in a lot of these cases. Many of the police officers that respond to the scenes of these calls report to their supervisors, who then make vital decisions in the circumstances, for example, whether an arrest should be made. There may be a lot of frustration among police officers because of how different police departments or key people (like supervisors) respond to calls about domestic violence. (Johnson 2004). Supervisors' bad attitudes and lack of consistency made it hard to enforce laws fully against domestic violence (Johnson 2004).

A third factor that affects police officers and their ability to manage domestic violence cases effectively is that they cannot control what happens after the arrest is made. Although police officers do control who is arrested and who is not, once the arrest is made, the only participation they have in the process is the potential as a witness. Police officers may not like how the rest of the criminal justice system deals with cases of domestic violence. After talking to the victim and the offender and figuring out who was the main aggressor, cases often do not go any further. Research from the past shows that officers are annoyed by the lack of action by prosecutors. (Toon & Hart, 2005; Blaney, E. 2005)

It is also important to mention that there has been research to suggest some police officers' attitudes toward domestic violence still could use improvement. Part of the issue could be that police officers have a tough time understanding why victims respond in specific ways, such as staying in bad relationships (Johnson 2004). These attitudes toward victims may cause the officers to become frustrated and display unjust outcomes toward the victims (Johnson, 2004; Toon & Hart, 2005). However, domestic violence advocates, victims, and officers assert that training can improve law enforcement responses, and multiple studies have found that police attitudes are capable of change, and training is one approach to facilitate attitudinal change (Toon & Hart 2005; Garner 2005; Blaney 2010).

Judicial Branch

I was also able to speak to two retired judges. It is tough to interview judges for things such as those presented in this dissertation because sitting judges cannot do anything to give the appearance of partiality towards people or issues and must apply the laws to the facts of each case. In doing an interview such as this one, individuals could argue that the judge cannot be fair and impartial on specific issues, thereby causing the need for them to be recused from some instances or, in the extreme, removed from the bench. Retired judges, however, do not have these restrictions and can speak freely. The two I talked to, with one serving in the State Circuit court and the other on the Supreme Court of Florida, provided a comprehensive overview of problems faced by members of the judiciary. The results suggest that even in situations where judges are educated on domestic violence issues, a lot of other factors affect how individuals are treated within the criminal justice system.

One of the significant factors that affect judges and their ability to do their job is the same one that affects all actors in the criminal justice system: the law. Judges are responsible for following the law, whether they agree with it or not. This means a judge must try to completely set their personal feelings aside, limiting their ability to effect change. As stated earlier, a Florida study in the *Sarasota Herald* found that there are definitely inconsistencies in sentencing (Braga 2022), but for individual judges, it can be challenging to understand what role they play in all of this. When I interviewed former judge George, who spent over 30 years on the bench as a state trial court judge, including more than seven years as a circuit criminal judge, he was asked about this ability to follow the law and stated, "My personal feelings often disagreed with the stated public policy goal, and yet I was obligated, consistent with my oath, to follow the law. And I did, but that's not to say I liked it." This sentiment of lacking control was shared at the Supreme Court level by former Supreme Court Justice Helen, who served as an Assistant Attorney General before moving to the Supreme Court and ultimately serving as Chief justice. In response to the question about her ability to follow the law, despite her personal feelings, "I am bound to follow the law, whether I like it or not. And there are always occasions when you think, what in the world is this law on the books? But as long as the law is there, you have to apply it...if I believe that it was constitutional, there's nothing I can do at that point but apply the law as it is, as it is. And so sometimes that's a little bit frustrating, but you do what you took your oath to do."

On a similar note, *Marbury v. Madison* explained the role of the court as having the ability to review governmental action and strike down those that are contrary to the Constitution. Like the other branches of government, these powers have been expanded and modified since their inception. However, the Courts are supposed to interpret the law and strike down laws that are not constitutional. However, they do not make laws, even though what constitutes making a law is up for interpretation. Some scholars even suggest that judges cannot and do not simply interpret laws to arrive at a "correct" answer. When asked about the separation of powers, George stated the Constitution of the United States and the Constitution of the state of Florida absolutely provide for a separation of powers. "Certainly, in the state of Florida, I would argue that the judiciary is the redheaded stepchild of those three, the separate and unequal branches of government." This sentiment is due in part to the fact that the judiciary is the only branch of government that does not actively participate in the budget for the state (or country), leading us to our next issue.

Judges also have to deal with a lack of resources to run a court efficiently. Jobs like court reporters, clerks' offices, and government attorneys are funded by the state's budget. A lack of money can cause more work due to fewer workers and higher caseloads. Additionally, expert witnesses through the public defender's office are funded by the state budget (Peng 2015). Smaller budgets mean that individuals are not receiving the justice they deserve through the criminal justice system. George explained, "With an insufficient budget and with insufficient support, the legislature and the governor have decided, and I'm referring to the legislative branch and the executive branch for our great state, have decided that we, the judiciary, will get what we get and what they determined we should have, which is a small pittance of the state budget." A smaller budget leads to the next issue of case management.

Another issue has been the COVID-19 pandemic. The pandemic has caused a backlog in the Florida court system, and the Supreme Court has noticed this problem and tried to fix it by imposing additional deadlines for judges to try to help resolve cases in both criminal and civil court. Many judges have expressed their dissatisfaction with these mandates. George stated, "By the same token, we are called upon to decide cases in a timely manner. And, of course, the new differentiated case management orders from our Florida Supreme court mandating various deadlines, pattern after the federal courts where the federal judges have, I won't say, an unlimited budget, but an expansive budget with two to three law clerks per judge, obviously a much different situation. So, there are simply insufficient resources for the state court trial judges to truly deal with this glacier of pending litigation in every division and obviously provide to the litigants both justice and finality." This leads to the issue of time.

Another issue that has been mentioned many times before is that of time. In many circumstances within the criminal justice system, there just simply are not enough hours in the day. A lot of these issues, especially issues that are novel and of first impression before the court, require training and education in order to understand them. However, that training is just not possible when a court division sometimes has close to 3,000 cases at a time. This number is based on the State Attorney's Office report of 60,228 total cases in 2017 and the 17 criminal divisions in the 13th Judicial Circuit. (Judicial Directory; State Attorney). Even from the Supreme Court level, Helen was able to recognize this and stated, "In the trial court level, the sheer number of cases, I think, makes it very difficult to ensure that each case really is given the kind of time and attention that it should be given."

It is essential to mention that although trial courts have extremely high caseloads, not all laws that adversely affect women (or anyone) actually make it to court. Someone has to be adversely affected, and the case has to make it into the Court system. As we have mentioned, in cases where victims refuse to cooperate with law enforcement, that can be difficult. However, judges cannot effectuate change unless the matter comes before them. Helen explained, "Someone's gotta be, um, adversely affected, basically. So, what does it mean? You go out...get arrested, and then you can test the constitutionality of it. And so that's sort of putting people in jeopardy unnecessarily." This is important because unless police officers make an arrest *and* prosecutors file charges, judges really have no power in cases involving women who have been the victim of physical violence. Then, as patients go through the appellate courts, the number of points that can be heard becomes smaller and smaller, leading us to our next issue.

Although trial courts have high caseloads and not much time, if they do not make the right decision, not all of the cases can be appealed. The benefit of appellate courts is that they usually have more time, but their authority is limited. When asked about the jurisdiction of the Supreme Court of Florida, Helen described, "Well, the jurisdiction of the Florida Supreme Court is limited. You cannot bring a case to the Supreme Court simply because you want to, under the Constitution. There are areas that you can bring to the Supreme Court. "A case has to come through us through a party. So, if there is someone who is adversely affected by a law, then they can bring a lawsuit, and hopefully, it will work its way to the Supreme Court. But we can't; I don't care how egregious I may have thought a piece of legislation was, I did not have the authority, the court, none of us on the court would have the authority to say, 'Let's take that case.'"

Further, appellate courts operate on panels of judges, so there is not one judge deciding a case. Therefore, even if you have judges that are educated and trained on issues, unless they all have a similar conclusion, the opinion of one judge could be irrelevant. Helen discussed this when asked about her personal power or opinion while on the Supreme Court "Well, it (the opinion) really didn't have any real weight or power because the majority said (otherwise)."

The last area that is important to mention is politics and the role that it plays in the judicial process. Although in Florida, there are some trial court seats that can be filled through the election, the appellate courts are all filled by appointments made by the governor. This usually means that principles and ideas that align with the governor's wishes, whatever those are, are put on the bench. Therefore, this process can be very political, and although judges are supposed to be non-partisan, a lot of issues that come before the court require rulings that will be affected by the judges' biases and perceptions (Biwer 2019). As Hope said, "And then you also have judges while they are supposed to be the factfinders, and they're supposed to, you know, justice is blind, they're human beings as well. They have their own biases; they have their own prejudice; they have their own thoughts." Therefore, when governors (like presidents) have the power to make multiple appointments to the court, the results, on many occasions, are political leanings in a specific direction. Helen discussed this in more detail, "It (a judicial appointment) certainly is because they have a certain ideology, there are certain things that they want to do, there're certain interpretations of the Constitution and, and laws that they feel are appropriate. And so, there are litmus tests in order even to be put on the bench these days. And so, I think we are headed down a perilous path, and I don't know how we get away from it except by voting for people who don't believe in those kinds of principles." This leads us to the discussion of the third branch of government, the legislative branch.

Legislative Branch

The legislative branch is one that oftentimes is overlooked. Although many times we suggest problems with laws, individuals, such as me, do seem to leave out the process of how rules get changed. Speaking to individuals who are involved in the legislative process has been eye-opening, to say the least. There are 120 legislative members of Florida's Congress—40 in the Senate and 120 in the House of Representatives. To pass a law or an amendment to the law means convincing most of those people that your solution is correct. This would be difficult for individuals who thought the same, so for people who come from diverse backgrounds, it seems impossible in many circumstances, not to mention the other issues that are involved in the other branches of government. It appears that, in many ways, my proposal to fix the laws will be the most difficult.

The most significant part of the legislative process that affects change is politics. Legislators are the individuals who are most commonly referred to as "politicians." Many of them have raised campaign funds and garnered votes on their platforms; therefore, when they get into office, they try to uphold those same platforms, whether right or wrong. When I asked Hope about the politics of the legislature, she said, "It's very partisan. I also say that if you are not a Republican white, straight cis-gendered man that has money, it is probably one of the most violent places you can be like mentally and emotionally." Many times, if a politician does not support the ideology or legislation of their donors and supporters, they cannot raise funding. She continued, "I have brought money home, but I'm about passing policy, and I've been able to pass policy that I'm passionate about, but there's a cost that comes with it, right? There's a cost of saying, listen, like I'm not going just to let you do and say anything and not, and take a walk or what, I'm not going to let you do that."

Lobbyists, in short form, are individuals charged with holding politicians accountable for their political platforms. The last person I interviewed was Irene. Irene is a young USF (University of South Florida) graduate who has been in politics since college and now runs her own successful political consulting firm, where she assists progressive candidates in achieving political success. When asked what a lobbyist is, she stated, "Lobbying is a job or a role, but a lot of people come to that space competing for different ideas and priorities. And so, I think that especially union organizations, law enforcement organizations, the NRA, all of these kind of really politically influential groups, kind of weigh in heavily on these members (legislators) to either act or not act on some of these issues, particularly SYG." The implication for these politics is that if you are not in the majority party, your voice cannot be heard. The issues that are important to you cannot be addressed. When asked how issues make the agenda to be discussed by politicians, she explained, "it's also relative to the pleasure of the member, right? I think you have some legislators who believe that this (SYG) is a critical issue year-round, no matter what happens, and they filed the bills, but going back to, if you're in the minority party, what's the likelihood of your bill being heard on this issue, and so can you even have the conversation in committee, if it doesn't get a hearing, it can be filed, and that's great, but if there's no political appetite for it, it makes it difficult to move those conversations." This segues us to the process of passing a law.

The entire process of getting a law passed can pose difficulties for members of the legislature, even when they are trained and educated on these complicated issues. Irene explained, "There are different political tactics. So, for instance, in the Florida legislature, you need to take a bill that needs to either come out of a committee or is filed both by a house member and a Senate member, at least for a bill to become law eventually. And so, if that happens...and those in the majority don't want to hear it, that means it will never go to the first committee stop, and nine times out of 10, they have to go through a couple of those before they go to the floor for a hearing. A political workaround is said you have another kind of relative bill; then you can tack on an amendment that could address that. But again, you can have that amendment heard, and they get voted down because of partisan politics. So, the process doesn't avail itself to healthy public policy debates, really, especially if there's not a balance of political power in the system."

Along the same lines as politics, many legislators are ambitious. They know that in order to progress in their careers, they have to take certain political stances. This makes it much more difficult for the legislators who actually care. Hope (who, again, is also a defense attorney) explained how she could tell the overly ambitious politicians, "It's (their ambition) very evident by the way they speak on the floor, by the votes that they take by the legislation that they pass. Very. And it's obvious that some of them are like, 'this is just a stepping-stone, this is just whatever, and especially if it doesn't personally impact them. It's whatever. This is a problem because when political actors do not take these issues seriously and personally, they are not likely to effectuate change, and the ones who do take these issues personally are impeded from making a change. She was also asked how she deals with the adversity of being a queer-black woman in politics, and she stated that she was "definitely constantly faced with adversity. And I chose not to leave it at the door. I believe that policy should be personal. I believe that you should take it personally. And if you're not taking it personally, I think that you shouldn't be in the legislature. You shouldn't be making policy. You have to understand that everything that we vote on, everything that we propose, it's going to affect someone's life, good, bad, or indifferent." This is important because for an issue to be addressed, lawmakers must think it is relevant, and if they do not take these issues seriously and personally, nothing will be suitable. As it relates to this research in particular, because these antiquated laws are based on white-heteronormative ideals that do not seem to be a concern in today's society, the issues are not likely to be viewed as relevant and, therefore, not possible to change.

Another problem with the executive branch is that the legislature is only in session for a brief period of the year. It is not a continuous thing. This limited time period means that not every issue can be addressed. Research suggests only the problems that are most important to the political agendas of the congress members get addressed (Barberá, P et al., 2019) (. When Irene was asked about the likelihood of reform to the SYG laws, she stated, "I think that it (SYG) only comes up in proximity to another issue, right? We don't have conversations just about violence to protect women, period. Domestic violence comes up in the conversations of gun safety, like what that means for red flag laws and things like that; or, for instance, that with the overturn of *Roe v. Wade,* Florida passed the 15-week abortion ban, then we talked about sexual violence. In the most egregious cases, if women want to seek out abortions, if they have a baby by way of rape or incest or something. So generally, on its face, we don't have those conversations about how we can improve or roll back laws for women or, no matter what their gender is, who are experiencing violence." The idea of relevance works against women who have been the victim of violence and SYG because that topic just is not relevant to the legislature to be discussed, let alone changed. First, SYG as it relates to IPV is not as common as other types of violence, and more importantly, there are few organizations more powerful than the NRA and ALEC which take an opposite stance on these issues (Bellassai 2012). Irene explained, "I think to SYG came up a lot in response to the murders of black people by law enforcement, right? I can't say that that conversation comes up outside of that."

A final factor that is important to mention is the governor. Since America operates under the principles of separation of powers, even if a lawmaker can convince the rest of the legislature to make or change a law, the governor can veto it, and it is clear that the current governor believes SYG is a good law since he championed an expansion to the law last year under the "COMBATTING VIOLENCE, DISORDER and LOOTING and LAW ENFORCEMENT PROTECTION ACT.." However, women were not included in any of the expansion provisions. In discussing the role of the current governor of Florida, Hope explained, "I think the governor is the architect of this; the governor rules by fear. I've spoken to Republican colleagues who have told me that directly. He rules by fear. He rules in a way that if you don't do what he wants, you will get 'primaried' [Opposition from the same party that runs against the lawmaker in the primary election], or you won't get your appropriations. He's very integral in this process, and he's doing it in an unprecedented way." Fear of repercussions from the governor could cause individuals with otherwise good intentions to rule contrary to their better judgment. A future area of study should be related to the effects of the governors' actions and women of physical violence.

Analysis

The interviews conducted for this Chapter provide multiple vital takeaways. Although some of the information was specific to domestic violence, most of the key takeaways can be applied to the criminal justice system overall. Additionally, many of these interviews referred to women who have been the victims of physical violence as victims in the system instead of defendants like they would be if they were charged with a crime for using self-defense. That point is critical to the analysis because it shows the standard way of thinking for criminal justice actors is women as victims. For these nuanced cases where women are defendants, criminal justice actors on all levels would have to re-program the way they traditionally think in order to apply the law to the facts of the case. These issues are not routine and require extensive training and experience, which takes time, time that these actors in the criminal justice system simply do not have.

Ultimately, we know that there are actors at all levels who do not understand the issues presented by women who have been the victims of violence and self-defense laws. We can see that the law is unequally applied to women, especially black women. However, this analysis will assume all of the actors in the criminal justice system have good intentions and want to ensure justice for all parties involved. This assumption is a significant stretch. However, the point of it is to show that even if we can change the attitudes of these actors, the results would likely still be the same.

Separation of Powers

Along the same lines as the previous point, the separation of powers within the system creates an issue in applying the law evenly throughout the criminal justice system. One of the most exciting aspects of the American government is the separation of powers. The Constitution is designed to prevent any one branch (or person) from having the ability to control our entire country. While this idea is good, in theory, it creates many problems in the application of our laws. In many of these cases, we see that the branches of government are not acting on one accord. While in some ways this is the desired effect, it also creates problems, mainly for the defendants. For example, as illustrated in Chapter 3, between 2010 and 2017, the legislative and judicial branches went back and forth over whether the prosecution or defendant would have the burden of proof in pre-trial immunity hearings under SYG. While this does not seem like an exceptionally long time, the effect was that prosecutors and defense attorneys in the executive branch constantly had to re-evaluate cases based on the changes in the law. This resulted in a lot of variations in sentencing for the same crime. This is a constant issue when the legislature makes laws that are hard to interpret by the judiciary or enforce by the executive branch. The implication of this is that even when we see changes in the direction that could be beneficial to women who have been victims of physical violence, if the laws are not clear to enforce or interpret, we will see little to no change to the results in these cases.

Lack of Agency

The existing structure of the American government system has created broader impacts for criminal justice actors than just a lack of direction. Another problem that was revealed by these interviews was a lack of ability to create change experienced by any of the actors. Many of the individuals I interviewed were, in fact, well-versed in issues surrounding women who have been victims of physical violence, yet many of them still felt powerless to change their impact on the system. For example, Hope stated that many times when advocating for issues to get pushed through the legislative process, she would have panic attacks during the process. Many other interviewees discuss the heavy burden placed on them when trying to handle cases and do the right thing. However, what we can see through the outcomes in the system, is that it is still working to disadvantage women, especially black women who use self-defense.[1]

Lack of Accountability

Due to the lack of agency or ability to create change, one of the biggest problems that these interviews illustrated within the criminal justice system is the lack of accountability of the criminal justice actors. In every single interview, except those done with legislative actors, the interviewee pointed to at least five problems in the system that did not involve the specific job to which they were assigned. In almost every case, those problems were legitimate. However, the temptation becomes to blame those other factors instead of looking internally for a solution. For example, prosecutors routinely stated that they could only make specific determinations for a defendant's mitigating circumstances based on what information was given to them about the defendants since defendants have a right to remain silent. While the right to remain silent does present an obstacle for prosecutors, in many cases, this can be an excuse not to do due diligence about the defendants' circumstances.

As another example, the judges routinely stated that they are charged with following the law, whether or not they agree with it. While this fact is absolutely actual, in theory, and likely does place limitations on the judge's ability to intervene in cases, when convenient, it also provides judges with an excuse to find deviations in sentencing guidelines for White defendants who can prove mitigating factors, such as mental health issues, that may not be present for Black defendants.

One way to combat this problem is with diverse committees, such as the homicide committee mentioned by Ellen. She described the committee as "a committee that's made up of the state of the elected state attorney, as well as all of the division chiefs at the state attorney's office. And it's a committee that meets on a weekly basis for a few purposes, mainly to review and make plea negotiations on all homicide cases at the state attorney's office. So, all homicide cases where an offer is going to be conveyed have to go through the homicide committee. And then there, the homicide could also be, we'll evaluate cases, homicide cases for filing decisions, whether we can file charges, from law enforcement who presents them. When you look at things like evidence issues, proof issues, the assertion of SYGs." She said the purpose of that committee is two-fold "to try to have some kind of consistency. I think as part of the reason for the homicide committee to try to have, you know, different perspectives represented, it's some people will see something a certain way." This could help to combat unequal treatment of cases by the prosecutor's office, but if it is not being done for every charge on every issue, it still is not compelling enough.

The only place where this lack of accountability was missing was in the legislative interviews, but only to an extent. During the legislative interviews, the interviewees were more likely to blame the lawmaking process or their fellow lawmakers, as opposed to the other branches of government. This is likely due to the vast number of individuals in the legislature, often with very opposing views, which makes it a lot easier to blame the other members. The problem, however, still remains, there is a lack of self-accountability which leads to a lack of personal change.

The implication of the lack of accountability is that in any given case where we see the law is unequally applied, as we saw in the circumstances in chapters 3 and 4, criminal justice actors do not take any lessons away from the cases because they do not attribute the failures in the system to individuals doing the same job as them. While every role likely has supervisors and trainers (except judges), those trainers are looking at problems on a smaller scale instead of looking at the system as a whole and figuring out what part they play in a solution.

Local and State Politics

Another factor that is always going to be prevalent in the criminal justice system is politics. At both the state, local, and national levels, politics is inextricably intertwined with the criminal justice process. In the legislature, the issue is clear. Lawmakers have to raise funds in order to be able to run for election. Those funds are necessary for the lawmaker to run a campaign; campaigns help lawmakers get votes, which is how they get elected. In raising those funds for election, almost all lawmakers make promises to their donors that they are going to uphold specific values and principles when elected. Those values and principles usually align with what the donor wants, whether that is justice and fairness or not. Therefore, when a lawmaker is selected, they support ideologies based on what their donors want so they can stay in office or if they are ambitious, progress to the next office.

Politics are also present in the executive branch since the governor, lead prosecutors, and lead public defenders are all elected to office. The same principles apply to these offices as they do to lawmakers. These individuals have to raise funds to campaign and also rely on votes. Therefore, they are likely to make decisions based on what the voters want, whether that is in the best interest of justice or not.

Unfortunately, the judicial branch is not immune to this concept either. Trial court judges can be elected or appointed, while appellate court judges are all appointed by the governor. This means that judges are either liable to the voting public or usually have the same ideology as the governor, who is also susceptible to the voting public. Therefore, when we have individuals in power who do not value doing what's in the interest of justice and fairness or considering issues surrounding implicit bias, critical gender theory, or critical race theory, we will likely see rulings from the court that reflect this. This is a sad reality since the judiciary is supposed to be non-partisan, but the fact of the matter remains that most people in our American capitalist society are loyal only to money.

Since politics have seeped into every fiber of the criminal justice system, it is hard to tell which cases are decided based on the laws and facts and which ones are political. It is highly likely that the more notoriety a patient receives, the less likely they are to be based on principles that are unrelated to politics.

Arbitrary Decision Making

Systemic implicit bias can be defined as the way that automatic racial bias may have become unintentionally mixed into and even mentally inseparable from legal theories that should be race-neutral (like retribution or rehabilitation) and approach to well-thought-out constitutional doctrines.

Systemic implicit bias shows that there is bias in the criminal justice system before a police officer decides to stop and search a person and before procedures like the death qualification of capital juries let bias into the trial process. Because people automatically think that Black lives are less important than White lives and that Black Americans need to be punished, bias is built into the system from the start when policymakers are deciding where to police and how aggressively, why to punish, and how much. Because of these things, implicit bias in the system can affect the decisions that elected prosecutors, police chiefs, and lawmakers make about policy. (Levinson & Smith 2016)

We recognize, from the existing research, the legal analysis, and the interviews, that implicit bias does exist and needs to be combatted. This factor is one of the significant contributors to injustice in the criminal justice system. However, even if all of the actors were trained and could put their biases aside so that they were applying the laws equally, the system still would not change because the structure of the system functions independently of individual preferences to disadvantage minorities.

The goal of this Chapter was to explain the inconsistencies between cases in Chapters 2 and 3 and how to remedy the issues presented in Chapter 1 by interviewing actors in the criminal justice system and learning the root causes of these problems. What the research shows is threefold: 1. the bias against women who have been the victim of sexual and other types of physical violence, especially black women, will not be remedied in the existing criminal justice system. 2. Changing the law will not ameliorate the problem. While it may have some effect, existing cases demonstrate that arbitrariness and bias are still embedded in the system. 3. Since the law does not administer itself; actors, including justices, attorneys, and juries, are forced to operate in a system that has implicit biases against women, even when individual actors educate themselves.

Discussion and Conclusions

The criminal justice system has proven to be a major hurdle for women who have been the victim of violence in the United States. This most commonly occurs because women who have been the victims of violence are either not believed or they are faced with extraordinary obstacles before they can receive help. Many women are reluctant to involve the justice system in any capacity for a multitude of reasons. Therefore, many women choose to endure the abuse in silence. However, in some circumstances women choose to defend themselves against the abuse. This dissertation has shown that in those situations, women still are not able to receive the protection that they deserve.

The introduction of Stand Your Ground laws in Florida seemed to be a way for more people to defend themselves against the threat of violence without facing repercussions from the legal system. However, this has only been the result for certain groups of people, usually White males, while other historically disenfranchised groups, such as Black people and women, remain disenfranchised even under these new laws.

The purpose of this study was to provide additional evidence to the growing body of research involving Stand Your Ground laws and the research surrounding Intimate Partner Violence. Although some studies have addressed Stand Your Ground laws as they relate to victims of Intimate Partner Violence, this research addressed multiple limitations, including addressing these laws as they relate to Black women specifically, and providing a real world approach through interviews with actors in the criminal justice system. The overarching goal was to establish the deep-rooted problems with the Stand Your Ground laws and with the criminal justice system as it relates to women who have been the victim of violence. This research will be critical for future policy reform by advocating for an intersectional approach with key actors from every branch of government.

Legal Analysis

The first area of study for this dissertation was through an in-depth legal analysis. This analysis began with the early suggested language of Stand Your Ground laws that appeared in Judicial opinions in the 1800s. From there, it explored the development of the Castle Doctrine, which was the first official "no duty to retreat" law and applied to individuals protecting their homes. From there, we can see that even within the Castle Doctrine, the patriarchal notions of men being the protectors of their home and women being property emerging through the areas of expansion and limitations of this law.

The Castle Doctrine has been expanded in places where men have been perceived as protecting their family from intruders. On the other hand, the Castle Doctrine has been limited in cases where women seem to be protecting themselves from abuse of a co-inhabitant. The rationale for this distinction appears to come from the idea that in the cases involving women, both parties have a legal right to be in the home, therefore in order to grant the wife immunity under this doctrine, the law would have to grant her superior rights in her own home. However, this logic does not seem to be based in sound principle, because in many of these cases, the woman has been able to establish that the co-inhabitant man was a perpetrator of abuse against her. Therefore, by not granting the woman immunity, our laws are, in many ways, granting the abuser superior rights by punishing a woman who acts in self-defense.

From the development of the Castle Doctrine, we have seen two separate and unequal trends emerging. For men, Stand Your Ground laws have developed as an expansion of the Castle Doctrine by applying the same principle to areas outside of the home. While this concept can also be applied to women, in theory, research shows women need protection within their own home. The law that has developed for these situations has been based on Battered Woman Syndrome, which is not even in itself a defense. A woman who defends herself in her home now has a two-fold burden to first show that she was the victim of abuse, then show that she was suffering from Battered Woman Syndrome, then finally show that her actions were reasonable in light of those conditions. On the other hand, when a man gets into a fight with a stranger, he only needs to show that he was in fear of harm or injury. These inequalities in the law serve as part of the reason women cannot get the justice that they deserve within the criminal justice system.

Case Analysis

The second area of study for this dissertation focused on Black women. This Chapter examined the stories of nine Black women to illustrate the many ways that Black women are forced to overcome hurdles within the criminal justice system in order to receive results similar to their White male counterparts. Ultimately, this Chapter demonstrates that even when these women do receive a "break" it is still not the same as the results of White men.

The Chapter starts with an example of the abuse Black women endured during slavery, when women had no rights. However, as the stories progress, we can see that even with "rights" the results were the same. Black women have to overcome society, juries, stigmas, placation, the past, the law, being a Black woman in America, and even the Battered Woman Defense. What these stories tell us is no matter how Black women are treated they are still expected to abide by laws that do nothing to protect them, and although they cannot call anyone to help them when faced with trauma or abuse, when they violate any of the traditional societal understandings for how they should behave, they will be subject to the full force of the law's punishment.

A major takeaway from this Chapter should be that the lack of protection received by Black women under the law should serve as an explanation of their distrust of the system. There is not a single case mentioned in this Chapter that serves as an appropriate response to the abuse these women endured. They were all either arrested or killed, even when their abuser suffered no injuries. There is nothing in these stories that would signal to a Black woman dealing with abuse that she could find any level of safety or recourse in the criminal justice system, and for that, we are failing these women.

Interviews

In the final area of study for this dissertation, interviews were conducted with key actors in the criminal justice system to determine how to fix the problems identified throughout the rest of the dissertation. These interviews included every branch of government and focused on finding solutions. However, that seemed like an impossible task.

The results of the interviews are threefold: 1. the bias against women who have been the victim of sexual and other types of physical violence, especially black women, will not be remedied in the existing criminal justice system. 2. Changing the law will not ameliorate the problem. While it may have some effect, existing cases demonstrate that arbitrariness and bias are still embedded in the system. 3. Since the law does not administer itself; actors, including justices, attorneys, and juries, are forced to operate in a system that has implicit biases against women, even when individual actors educate themselves.

The results of this study present several implications for current research and policy. First, Stand Your Ground laws must be revised to include protections for women who have been the victim of violence. Florida is not the only state with Stand Your Ground laws based on white, patriarchal, heteronormative ideals of what it means to defend one's person, property or family. This makes sense because a lot of these laws are enacted at the legislative level through private funding of right winged conservative groups like the NRA and ALEC (Ferriss, 2012; Sloan 2012). This research will not delve into that aspect of Stand Your Ground laws because no matter who is behind these laws the intent and effect become dangerously clear through their application. In looking at these laws and the differences between them, the point remains the same: this country has not gotten to a place where our laws on self-defense protect women from violence. The common theme in all these laws is that women are an afterthought. In some states, because of their gender, the pronouns of the laws are not even inclusive.

Second, any changes to these laws must include actors from every branch of government to ensure that change is occurring. Change cannot occur if the laws are revised, but the judiciary does not interpret them appropriately; or if the judiciary makes a correct interpretation but prosecutors find new ways to file charges or refuse to dismiss cases. Ultimately, this problem is much broader than a single solutions and policy development must account for this fact.

Finally, these findings show that policy on self-defense laws must include provisions to protect Black women. This research has shown that the positionality of Black women at the intersection of two historically oppressed groups make it extremely difficult to receive justice. Further, multiple studies have shown, and cases have implied that some of these women are not only Black, but they are also poor, which adds an additional level of oppression within the criminal justice system. These women have been marginalized for too long and current trends for reducing sentences and granting clemency to women who are proven victims of human trafficking is not doing enough. Instead, it is creating a guise of justice that causes our society to maintain a false sense of equality, while still punishing these women. Future policy needs to account for these women and protect them.

Strengths and Limitations

This dissertation is the first known examination of Stand Your Ground laws and Intimate Partner Violence that places a specific focus on Black women and the abuse that they have endured. Multiple studies have examined Stand Your Ground laws as they relate to Intimate Partner Violence (Crisafi 2016; Coker, 2014; Franks, 2014; Johnson, 2015; Suk, 2008), however they focus on all women and do not specifically address issues surrounding Black women. By examining popular and lesser-known cases involving Black women, I have demonstrated the various institutional mechanisms that disadvantage these women within the criminal justice system.

Further, this dissertation is the first known examination of Stand Your Ground laws and Intimate Partner Violence that includes interviews with current and former practitioners too provide a solution. These interviews have shown that the many different aspects of a case in the criminal justice system allows individuals to deflect blame to other individuals and cause change to be much slower. Furthermore, even the actors with the most experience and best intentions are hamstrung by the policies and procedures that comprise our justice system. Therefore, even when these actors acknowledge the problems and want to create change, they are limited by the rules and also by political concerns in addition to the other stressors that come with doing their job efficiently and effectively.

The largest limitation on this study was the lack of available quantitative data. Multiple public records requests to all 20 Florida State Attorney's Offices confirmed that quantitative data related to Stand Your Ground laws specifically is not being retained, although Florida Statute 776.09 states:

> Whenever the state attorney or statewide prosecutor dismisses an information, indictment, or other charging document, or decides not to file an information, indictment, or other charging document because of a finding that the person accused acted in lawful self-defense pursuant to the provisions related to the justifiable use of force in this chapter, that finding shall be documented in writing and retained in the files of the state attorney or statewide prosecutor.

Therefore, many of the findings made in this dissertation could not be confirmed through statistical analysis.

Additionally, the cases that were examined likely display some level of bias, because they all either made national attention or were available through a judicial decision. This means that cases that resolved in a plea before trial, were dismissed by prosecutors before trial, or individuals who were not arrested by the police were not the subjects of this research. Once again, this is where the data that prosecutors should be maintaining would be very helpful. Therefore, this is hopefully a limitation that can be addressed by future research.

Another limitation on this study involves my positionality as a former prosecutor. The interviews that were conducted were all individuals that I know personally and have had a working relationship with, in some form. While I do not believe that the interviewees provided inaccurate information during the interviews, the situation was likely different in some ways because I was not a stranger. On the other hand, it is very likely that these interviewees may not have agreed to the interviews without that relationship because I have formed a level of trust with them. Further, it is important to mention that I likely have my own biases in this research as a former practitioner who was still currently a prosecutor when this project started.

Future Directions of Study

The findings of this study shows significant issues with the stand your ground loss as they relate to women who have been the victim of violence. At the forefront of future research should be quantitative analysis to show the desperate impact these laws are having on women as it relates to conviction rates and sentencing. These results will be imperative to show the importance of correcting these laws. This can be accomplished by requiring prosecutors to follow the law in maintaining data related to stand your ground laws. further the lack of records related to these cases raise questions about why the information is not being maintained. It is very possible that there is something contained in that data that would be very important to future research.

Future research should also include more data related to human trafficking and stand your ground. Human trafficking is becoming a nationwide issue and many of the cases involving black women arise based on issues dealing with human trafficking. Currently Florida's Stand Your Ground laws do nothing to address this group of women. Future research should look into these cases specifically in order to find a solution to protect these young girls from sexual predators.

The third area for future research should involve same sex couples. While this dissertation has focused on women who have been the victim of violence, it is important to note that intimate partner violence includes same sex couples as well. This dissertation did not have the resources available to be able to tackle that question, mostly due to the lack of existing cases regarding same sex couples. However, inclusivity within criminal justice should be a growing issue that works to address the individuals that comprise our society and the issues they may face, regardless of race, gender, or sexual orientation. All things considered, addressing these issues will provide stronger arguments in order to present policymakers and criminal justice actors with enough data to hopefully make corrections to this law.

www.ingramcontent.com/pod-product-compliance
Lightning Source LLC
LaVergne TN
LVHW010335200726
843507LV00010B/1498